# MARITIME
# OF NEWPORT
# PEMBROKESHIRE

The ANT, a ship built by Levi Havard in Newport Pembrokeshire in 1816. 130 tons Snow Rig. Seen here passing the original wooden built Smalls Lighthouse. Two years before, French privateers captured and held for ransom another Havard ship. As a deterrent, this ship was painted with gun ports to make her appear from a distance that she was armed. This was the first Newport ship to have painted ports and may have been the first British merchant ship to adopt this tactic against pirate attack.

# MARITIME HISTORY
## OF NEWPORT PEMBROKESHIRE

Castles, Inscribed Stones, Pilgrim Crosses, Shipwrecks Shipbuilding, Rowing Races, and Newport Nonsense.

© **TOM BENNETT 2019**

**ISBN:** 9781549713040

# CONTENTS

| | | |
|---|---|---|
| Introduction | *Page* | 5 |
| Edrywy | | 6 |
| Owens of Henllys | | 8 |
| Old King Cole | | 10 |
| Bowens of Llwyngwair | | 10 |
| Cromlechs and Inscribed stones | | 11 |
| Ogham | | 13 |
| Nevern Castle | | 14 |
| Toad Man of Trellyffaint | | 15 |
| Pentre Ifan | | 18 |
| St Brynach | | 18 |
| Seal Bay Saga | | 19 |
| Pilgrims | | 20 |
| Suspicions and Superstitions | | 23 |
| Sleeping Giant or Earth Goddess | | 25 |
| School of Navigation | | 26 |
| The Wells, Pystyll or Ffynnon | | 27 |
| Medieval Kiln | | 30 |
| Eco Centre and Sustainability | | 31 |
| Twinning of Towns | | 32 |
| Town Crier | | 33 |
| Unaccompanied Singing | | 34 |
| Court Leet | | 35 |
| The Coastline | | 36 |
| River Nevern | | 37 |

# Contents (continued)

| | Page | |
|---|---|---|
| Sewin & Salmon | | 37 |
| Llwyngwair Mansion | | 38 |
| Essex Havard | | 40 |
| Newport Surf Lifesaving Club. | | 42 |
| Early Shipping. | | 43 |
| Cwm yr Eglwys | | 45 |
| Lower Fishguard | | 56 |
| Newport Nonsense | | 63 |
| The Chain Crossing | | 65 |
| Culm | | 68 |
| The Pole | | 68 |
| Stephen, the Ferry Man | | 69 |
| Whales | | 70 |
| Ship Register and Tonnage | | 74 |
| Cargoes | | 78 |
| Rigs of Newport Built Ships | | 81 |
| Chronology of Ship Building, | | 84 |
| Newport Owned Ships | | 127 |
| Building Costs of a Schooner | | 158 |
| Voyages in 1870. | | 159 |
| Lifeboat House | | 162 |
| Oline and Desdemona | | 165 |
| More Shipwrecks | | 164 |
| Newport and its Rowing Tradition | | 168 |

**Contents** (continued)

Cardigan losses, from Newspapers  *Page* 177
Methodology used to get information        193

Index of Newport Vessels   A- C   185
Index of Newport Vessels   C- F   186
Index of Newport Vessels   F- J   187
Index of Newport Vessels   J- M   188
Index of Newport Vessels   M- S   189
Index of Newport Vessels   S- W   190
References                         192
Contact Me                         194

## INTRODUCTION

This is a book that I have been wanting to write for more than forty years. I fell in love with Pembrokeshire during my teenage years when enjoying summer holidays at Dale. Since 1970 I have lived at various locations around the county. Llysyfran, Goodwick, Dinas, Nevern, Newport, Llangwm, Pembroke Dock, Hazelbeach and Milford Haven. At each place attempting to assimilate as much history as I can of the localities I was living in. Countless hours have I spent in Archives and Reference Libraries reading about Pembrokeshire life and its sea-faring heritage. To get a feeling for its immense history, you must first read the accounts of Giraldus Cambrensis, Fenton, Timmins and Owen of Henllys.

To get a background of the political history you must understand who was who and the lineage of the older Pembrokeshire families, the Wogans, the Phillips, the Bowens, and those occupying the Manor houses and Castles and those seated in power.

There are only a handful of people who are keenly interested in the sizes and quantity of the brigs, sloops and schooners built on the banks of the Nevern nearly 200 years ago. Nevertheless there are many who take a casual interest in the subject. I fear that if I do not record the subject, the information will remain dormant in the archives, unseen and thus not be a part of the everyday knowledge of the locality. Regard this book not as an academic account but as a jigsaw of notes that I find of interest. I make no apologies for the digressions, they arrive in the text as I write, of what intrigues me, hopefully you may find some of them of interest too!

When reading the History of Newport in the Town's website I was intrigued to read that the Beach at one time was named Traeth Edrywy. Today the small rock off Pen Morfa is called Carreg Edrywy. William Lewis in 1747 marked it on a chart as both this name and merely "Edrywy". Without going into great detail, the name itself means 'New Town near the Beach' probably named about 1215.

The region of Nevern and Newport was one of the most important medieval areas of Wales. Indeed thousands of years before that the late Neolithic settled and farmed and the population was so large that Dinas (City) was so named, inferring a large religious population or gathering of people. Nevern was a meeting place for the Welsh Princes. Once a year there was a big festival with jousting, merriment and a horse fair. On 27th June Newport would celebrate Ffair Gurig a traditional horse trading day. The author believes that it was an occasion when the Irish would come over to Pembrokeshire bringing their horses to trade. Even today Nevern Show is regarded as an important occasion for horse lovers and is a legacy of what was happening there at least one thousand years ago.

There has always been a close connection between the Irish and the Welsh and it is often said that the Irish inhabited Pembrokeshire before the Welsh. Looking at the time 3900 BC-3600 BC there is much evidence to support this. The author is of the opinion that the ashes of the Newport elite throughout the Megalithic period were sent over to the tombs in the Boyne Valley because their ancestors had been buried there. There are carved kerbstones at Knowth that are carved in the same way as carvings seen on Mynydd Dinas.

***Carreg Coetan Arthur.*** A dolmen at the landing place at Newport. As much as a welcoming feature for the Irish and a statement of power and sophistication to foreigners as it is a burial place.

Primarily this book is intended to concentrate on maritime matters, but I will start by giving a hotchpotch of town and land history that you may not be familiar with.

**Standing stones, Celtic Crosses and Burial Chambers.**

Newport and Nevern have some of the richest density of inscribed stones, standing stones, cromlechs and Religious monuments in the whole of Wales.

There are no less than 6 Cromlech sites nearby ; Nevern. Pentre Ifan, Carreg Coetan Arthur, Cerrig y Gof, Trellyffaint, Llech y Dribedd, and Bedd yr Afanc.

**Carreg Coetan Arthur -** N 52° 01.115 W 004° 49.697 This Neolithic Burial Chamber has been dated to 3640 BC. If you do not have time or means to get to Pentre Ifan, then you must look at this dolmen. I have now accepted its setting amongst the 1980's buildings nearby, realizing this has helped to preserve this monument for the future. Its original purpose was a chamber in which the corpse of a important chief was defleshed, the first part of an elaborate funerary process. (See my book *Neolithic Pembrokeshire* for more). The word Arthur in its name can be ignored. Arthur is a corruption of the word *Bear* in Welsh which denoted a strong warrior. Nothing to do with either of the two King Arthurs who came along some 3000 years later.

Newport area has a number of other important archaeological sites One curious site, **Cerrig y Gof,** 52.013706N 4.862641W lies in a field next to the Dinas to Newport main. Its name can be translated to 'Smithy Stone' or 'Mound of Memories'. It consist of five chambers concentrically placed and all outward facing. The author knows of no other Megalithic structure like this in Wales. Although Y Gof means 'blacksmith' and charcoal and black sea pebbles were found on the site by Fenton in 1811, even he had his doubts about the chambers as being used as graves. It could have been built as a communal excarnation place but never used as such and its use changed. If not an early foundry the site was a place where 'sacred' charcoal was made, the very first export product from Dinas.

It lies on a line between Dinas Head, Needle Rock and Foel Drygarn, a line where other cysts lie.

Those studying Newport's unique history have a distinct advantage. Being a town with a King's Decree and a manorial base it has written records, second to none in the National Library of Wales. A Court Leet and a Court Baron, are ancient institutions that exist today as they have done so for 800 years. Records of these meetings go back centuries giving us details of who was the Lady Marcher, who was the Lord of the Manor and who was appointed Mayor of the Ancient Borough. In the 1960's when Dillwyn Miles was Mayor he resurrected the ancient custom of 'Beating the Bounds' to show the younger members of the community where the boundaries of the ancient borough extended to. The National Library of Wales even has a town map showing who lived in Long Street before the Castle was built in the 13th Century. This was extremely useful when Dyfed Archaeological Trust carried out a dig prior to the building of the new Ysgol Bro Ingli School. The archaeologists could work out the name of the occupier of the 13th century house they were digging up! Newport was also blessed with having some of the greatest writers and historians Pembrokeshire has seen residing near its borders. The Lords of the Manor, were amongst the Welsh elite. Their religious Protestant persuasions, their influence in Parliament and on land use and taxes, have moulded Newport and Wales into what we see today. The most influential persons of Newport and Nevern come from the very large Owens family that lived at Henllys. George Owen of Henllys (1552 – 26 August 1613) was a Welsh antiquarian, author, and naturalist. He was the eldest son to Elizabeth Herbert and William Owen. They lived in a Tudor manor house which is presently being excavated by the University of York. William Owen was a wealthy Welsh lawyer who purchased the Lordship of Kemys. At the time of George's birth, his father was 82. William Owen died at 102 years old in 1574. George Owen was educated in law at the Inns of Court in London and after many lawsuits took over the title of Lord of Kemys (Cemais). In 1571 he married Elizabeth Phillips of Picton Castle. Together they had no less than eleven children but another George Owen was a product of his second wife.

In 1578 Llwyngwair was occupied by a James Owen who had married Eleanore Griffith, granddaughter of Sir William Griffith, Knight of Penrhyn. He was one of the most powerful men in North Wales. These families shaped not only the development of Newport but of Wales as a whole.

As a precis of Newport history we move from Welsh Princes at Nevern Castle to Norman Knights at Newport Castle . A grant of land was given to a knight Cole who came from France with Martin de Tours and William The Conqueror. This land was at Llwyngwair. It would be nice to associate this Cole as a descendent of the French legendary figure 'Old King Cole, a merry old soul etc'. He was a keen agriculturalists and it is said with an auger from France, Cole studied the soils of the lands all the way down the west coast of Wales. Favourably impressed with the marl he found around Newport he chose his land at Llwyngwair. In 1326, William Cole was on a jury in Newport so we know he was living at Llwyngwair at that time. Sir James Bowen, adherent of Henry VII, bought the property from the Coles in 1503. Prior to that the family were living at Pentre Ifan. A timber vaulted roof structure still exists from the sixteenth century at Pentre Ifan.. James Bowen (the second) had no less than seventeen children, his eighth son emigrating to Boston, Massachusetts in 1640. For generations the Bowens of Llwyngwair were the feudal, 'Lord of the Manor', owning the farms and the mill adjoining. Great respect was given by the inhabitants of Newport to the Bowen's but it must be remembered that many of them were in their direct employ. What is not generally acknowledged is the enormous amount of landscaping that went on when Llwyngwair Manor was being built. Today as you approach there is a hump in the ground half way between the Lodge and the Mansion. This is a "Ha Ha" of sorts.

It was built to hide the view of those in the Mansion from seeing those passing on the Cardigan road. It would have been constructed without mechanical labour and is a considerable amount of soil to move using a horse, a cart and some shovels. All the woods and grounds around Llwyngwair were carefully designed and planted. Just like the grounds of Picton Castle, shrubs, trees and exotic plants from the far east and Mediterranean were specifically brought into Pembrokeshire for these gardens. Behind the mansion was an area made into a duck decoy, encouraging wild duck into an enclosed pond. Here wild duck could easily be captured for food. Duck oils were used for waterproofing boots and making leather supple, the feathers used for making feather beds. Hazel trees were planted to encourage woodcock and on the map we can see a Cockshut Wood. A line of Sweet Chestnuts were planted. Posts from these trees, do not rot in the ground. The Hazel woods were coppiced for firewood and fencing and certain oaks pollarded to provide grown knees for the shipbuilding. The sandy lane between the Mansion and Nevern Church was brushed clear of leaves every Sunday to allow the Bowens to go to Nevern Church by horse and trap. All the others working at the Mansion had to walk down the lane to Church, stopping to bow or courtesy and much doffing of hats as the trap passed by.

The Bowens were sympathetic to the Methodist movement. Between 1772 and 1777 it is known that John Wesley stayed at Llwyngwair Mansion at least six times. A large tree in the grounds, between the Mansion and the river, where he preached still exists. The Bowens in the nineteenth century, and the Lloyds of Coedmor still spoke Welsh. They understood the importance of not dispelling the Welsh language. Llwyngwair translates as a 'bundle of hay' or a 'grove of grass'. On the biggest tides the sea water reaches the grounds of Llwyngwair. In doing so it passes Felin Llwyngwair, the water mill that ground all the corn. Small ships could load here and wheat was once an important export of Newport.

At Llanllawer, above Llanychaer is a line of standing stones named **Parc y Meirw,** 'Field of the Dead'. There are other alignments in Wales but these have the tallest stones and some believe it can be used to calculate the next sun eclipse. The direction of the stones point to Wicklow the shortest sea crossing across St Georges Channel. From Mynydd Dinas on a clear day you can see both Snowdonia and the Wicklow Mountains. Indeed many of the cromlechs in West Wales seem to point to Ireland, perhaps a direction from whence their descendents had come from. Nevern Church has its Celtic Cross, one of the most elaborate in Wales. But dated late 10$^{th}$ or 11$^{th}$ Century is not as old as many believe, and it may be a copy of one from 300 years before. More ancient (c. 5$^{th}$ century) is the south window cill inside the Church that has both Latin and Celtic Ogham (Ogam) writing on it. Mathry Church also has such markings. The oldest stone inscriptions to be seen are on the Vitalianus Stone standing to the east of the porch. In the past this stone was removed from the north side of the Church to be used as a gate post at Cwm Gloyne, returned to the churchyard in the 1950's.

Some say that Ogham writing was taken to Ireland from Wales just before the introduction of Christianity. I always thought it was the other way around! To keep everyone happy, let us say it started in both places at the same time.

Ogham wrting was deciphered using the latin text of the Sacranus stone in the Nave of St Andrew's Church at St Dogmael's Abbey.

Henry's Moat Church and the church at Llanllawer both have these prehistoric crosses that must relate to Calendar alignment at least one thousand years before the Saints arrived.

## 5th or 6th Century Ogham writing in Nevern Church.

*Copyright: Martin Coleman 2018*

Nevern Church is built on land where the Irishman St Brynach established a chapel about 540 AD. Brynach and Padarn were both contemporaries of Saint David and it is said they all visited Jerusalem together. After being a missionary in Brittany, St Brynach moved to Login in Wales, where he was alienated. He then attempted to settle in the Gwuan Valley, but there too 'evil spirits' caused him to move on. Eventually he established himself in Nevern where he was accepted. Brynach is associated with churches at Cwm yr Eglwys, and Pontfaen in the Gwaun Valley. Other churches dedicated to him include those at Llanboidy, Cillymaenllwyd, Llanfrynach and Henry's Moat. The avenue of Yew Trees inside the Nevern Church boundaries are reputed to be 700 years old. The Yew tree provided the raw material to make the Welsh Long Bow. As the evergreen leaves and the yew berries are poisonous to cattle, horses, goats and sheep the trees were grown next to the churches, the boundary walls of the church yard preventing the animals from getting near to the trees. Giraldus in 1180 talks of Glamorgan archers using a short bow made of wych elm not of yew. Long bow seem to have come later and certainly by the 16th century long bows made of yew. The Welsh in the south were renowned for their archery. Nevern Yew trees could have made long bows for the Tudor navy in the 16th century. A replica of a yew longbow found on the **Mary Rose** shipwreck could shoot a 53.6 gram arrow some 328 meters. At short range they had the power to send an arrow through most body armour.

**Legends of Trellyffaint.**
The original folklore of Trellyfaint, a farm inhabited for more than a thousand years, is given by Giraldus Cambrensis in 1182. A chieftain, with the name of Cecil Longshanks, was being molested by toads, so much so that he became extremely ill. While he was being cared for, hundreds of toads turned up and threatened to climb all over him. His carers tried to get rid of the evil creatures but the more they killed, the more toads turned up. In desperation they made a cloth hammock and tied the man up in a high tree, hoping the toads would not reach him. "Nor was he there safe from his venomous enemies, for they crept up the tree in great numbers, and consumed him, even unto the very bones." Cecil ended up as a sackful of white bones. The fable continues that it is this chieftain's bones that are buried in the Trellyffaint cromlech. Roger also related a further story that he had gained from the elderly farmer living there. It was how to become a Toad-Man, a man blessed with special mystical powers over animals. If you want to become a Toad-Man with special powers over animals, you do the following. First you catch your toad and place it in an ants nest for a month to collect the clean bones. You take the bones down to the Camman brook, by Nevern Church and throw the bones into the running water one by one. Eventually one of the bones will swim, screaming, upstream against the river flow. This is the one you must catch and keep in your pocket for three days and nights. Each evening you must walk three time around the Trellyffaint burial chamber. Each night the devil will attempt to take the bone from you. On the third night if you still manage to retain the bone you can deposit it inside the chamber and make your wish. If that wish is to be a 'Toad-Man'. Then you will possess special powers, especially curative powers over animals. The old farmer told Roger that he had not tried it but his father in around 1890 had done so to become a Toad-Man, and it did help him care for his cattle.

This bone ritual relating to this burial site will go back many centuries before St Brynach established his monastery in Nevern. The fact that Girald Cambrensis mentions it in the 11th century as an old fable is significant. There are elements to the story that I recognize as going back to the religion of the Megalithic people. In late Neolithic times they believed that the frog or toad was the rebirth symbol. That all life started as a black spot in the Underworld and progressed into the sky or the Otherworld in the heavens. The frog was always climbing upwards and could reach the sky on the back of a bird or itself change into a bird to fly into the sky past the Cygnus Star to the Otherworld. Here the spirits or souls of the dead would reside until they were ready to be reborn. Frog spawn or a goose with the spirits would drop from the sky to land on the earth. This would contain the black dots of life or the spirits of the dead person who could start the cycle once again. The black dots of the tadpoles were symbolic of the tiny stones or ashes of the ancestors who were about to start life on earth again. It was a continuous Cycle of Life. Death was just the start of the Rebirth process and the spirits were contained in very small stones. Perhaps you can see why stones were so important to these Stone Age people. Not only were their tools made of stone but their descendents were embedded in the stones surrounding them. The megalithic people had no desire to live in caves or underground. Below ground level was the Underworld, not a hell, but a place which was difficult to get out of, a place where Lost Souls went. When I see in the story of Cecil Longshanks being eaten by toads it is the twist to the story that the monks of St Brynach have added. To try and dispel the Pagan religion they are making frogs into evil toads. The hammock in a tree with a bag of bones is similar to a sky burial or a defleshing of bones before burial. The story is an explanation of why bones are seen at ritual sites and that the Pagan funerary processes of rebirth are a 'load of rubbish'.

We still see strong views of 'Pagan rubbish'. It is this indoctrination of the Christian religion still trying to dominate our beliefs. This is why we see Isis fighters destroying museums and temples in an attempt to eradicate contrary ideologies. It is still seen in the archaeologists having no regard to those that believe in spirit lines. The Neolithic people lived in a spirit world and a material world. There was little difference between the two. It is unfortunate that modern man and certainly those living outside Asia have lost their spiritualism. Modern man relies on science, technology, legislation and money to sort out his problems, not understanding that common sense should be applied instead. It is sad this common sense is no longer available.

**Suspicions and Superstitions .**

This has triggered my memory into another story that must be mentioned. There is an old mansion called Trewern that has Elizabethan features and is thought to be mainly constructed around 1650. At the back of the house are the remnants of a cock fighting ring and suggestions of an earlier building. The Bowens lived there before moving to Llwyngwair. It was said that during Cromwell's time, (1660's) religious artefacts from St David's were removed from the Cathedral for their own safety and taken by horseback (one day's ride) to Trewern and hidden in the mansion. Around the 1920's on the renovation of Trewern a small secret room, above the main doorway, was broken into and the icons discovered. Then the three religious treasures, including a chalice and a golden figure, again mysteriously vanished. One of the ministers at the time (name withheld) moved to near Pen-Waun, on the road out of Nevern. He developed a twitch in his neck as though he was always looking behind him. Newport people were convinced that it was he who knew the whereabouts of the lost Trewern treasure. Did he sell the artefacts or are they still hidden somewhere near his house in the woods of Nevern?

St Brynach and his monastic mate, which included St David, used to sit on top of Carningli contemplating cosmic matters. (Note there is no reference source for this snippet of information, as required by academics).
Lawrence Main, the somewhat eccentric Vegan, believes that Carningli was revered as the home of the Earth Goddess in pre-Christian times. He is quite attuned to Ley lines which he prefers to call Spirit Lines. If you are interested in long distance walks then read his books. Carningli is one of his favourite sleeping places. Carningli was obviously a sacred place prior to St Brynach's arrival, probably predating him by a few thousand years.
On the Queen's Jubilee celebrations, I, like many others from Newport, lit a beacon on the high point of Carningli. It was only the other day I had my first look for Neolithic carvings on this elevated tor. Although easy walking it took me two hours to get the top from the middle of Newport Town and I must say I was quite exhausted when I got there. I found less carvings than I was expecting to find and no ancient cairn. On the way up you will see a variety of what I call 'pyramid stones'. These mark various lines across the landscape and I noticed that one line pointed from Needle Rock, through Cerrig y Gof, through Carnedd Meibion Owen and onto Foel Drygarn. This is the setting Sun position on the Mid Summer Solstice. Note this line does not touch the top of Carningli but skirts its lower northern slope. This suggests that the 5 cysts chambers at Cerrig y Gof are intermediary burial chambers built at the time when funerary processes were transitional between cremation and burial into the ground. Perhaps it was built as burial chambers but never used as such. The radial pattern of cysts showing that the direction of spirits of the dead was not of prime importance any more. This would date Cerrig y Gof to about 2500 BC, a date when the Bronze Age was being born.

**Pentre Ifan.** This dolmen, the most iconic of its type in Pembrokeshire is probably one of the last to be built. Unlike the tombs seen in Ireland most of the Welsh dolmens were never entirely covered with earth. They were built for the most important members of the community. On death the body was sewn into a seal skin blanket and placed inside this tomb which was then made inaccessible to foxes. Over the course of the next year the body gradually decomposed and was naturally defleshed by insects, worms and small rodents. Two stones were placed outside the dolmen. During this time some of the spirits or soul of the body could depart. After at least one year, the chamber sides were opened up and the corpse and bones, now naturally cleaned were taken out. The leather shroud now acting as a bag for dried bones. Family members would each take a small foot bone from the bag before it was ceremonially cremated on a high place. The cremation ritual was carried out at night on a mountain top near to the dolmen . The ashes flying into the sky was a metaphor for the spirits of the dead person ascending into the heavens. However if was vitally important that all the spirits had departed to the Other World. At the next All Souls day the ashes and stones and a bone from a previous ancestor were carried on a processional walk.

Newport's maritime history would not be complete without mention of the Seal Bay Saga.

Members of the Surf Lifesaving Club were doing an evening training exercise in 1983. To give the outboard engine a spin they took a trip up to Ceibwr in their Inshore Lifeboat. Seeing something hidden under tarpaulins they landed on a beach to have a look. A sheepish man emerged who was trying to make up a story that he was involved with training for an expedition to film whales in the Arctic. Customs and the local Police were informed who made enquires. Dinas people could tell them that lights had been seen flashing at night from a rented cottage above Spring Hill on Dinas mountain. Two local Police officers thought they had better investigate. On arrival near the cottage a man with a rucksack was seen panicking and running away across the fields shouting "don't shoot, don't shoot". The police were not armed but thought they had better arrest the fellow for questioning. The man was Soeren Berg-Arnback. A Dane, and the most wanted Drug Smuggler in Europe. In his rucksack was a high powered MF radio which the Police were to set up on the headland hoping for a signal with which to connect the man with an illegal act. Sure enough a midnight call came in to collect Class A drugs from a position in the St George's Channel, and bring them into a hideaway on Seal Beach. Only then were the Special Branch Drugs Squad informed much to their annoyance at being usurped by Pat Molloy and the local force. Unwittingly the biggest European Drug Smuggling Ring had been busted. Soeren, the man who was seen flashing £50 notes in the local pubs, received an eight year prison sentence. I was fortunate to see the wood and fibreglass man-made cave dug deep into the pebble beach, made waterproof by a yacht hatch at high water mark. It was obviously a cache for firearms or drugs, that must have taken months to construct.

*For more on this story read 'Operation Seal Bay' by Pat Molloy. ISBN 13:9780450531491. www.bbc.co.uk/programmes/p00krjws.*

In about 1972 there was a climber killed on the cliffs of Seal Bay. His buddy was very quick in departing from the scene. As the rope they were using was not a climbing rope I was always suspicious as to what they were up to. I knew the climbing cliffs of Pembrokeshire and Seal Bay is not one of them. At the time I thought it must be two men trying to steal Peregrine Falcon eggs or chicks. I now think these two men may have been part of the same smuggling ring and could have started making their artificial cave as early as 1972. That is eleven years before the Seal Bay Operation was busted.

The 6th to the 11th century is an interesting period in Pembrokeshire. It is the time when the Romans had departed and we are now only beginning to see what influence they had in the region. The Romans certainly built roads through Pembrokeshire and as we do not see elaborate villas, we must consider that the Romans regarded the area as a 'passing through' place. An area opposite Ireland, where their boats can import gold and copper from Ireland and Anglesey and transport it inland to places like Carmarthen and Caerleon. From the 6th century we see the arrival of Pilgrims passing through Nevern on their way to St David's or Ynys Enlli (Bardsey Island).

**Vikings**

In the 9th to 11th century we see Viking incursions and some settlement. Dublin, Cork, Limerick, Wexford and Waterford were true Viking towns and in the 9th century Hubba used Milford Haven as the base for his fleet of Viking longboats. I believe that there was a Viking settlement at Pencaer near Strumble Head. In the last few decades it is now known that they had a settlement at the north end of Anglesey, probably because, like the Romans, they needed the minerals from Parys Mountain.

*www.coflein.gov.uk/en/site/304307/details/cnwc-farmhousest-marys-church-newport-inscribed-stone*

If you are interested in inscribed stones dated 7th to 9th century then there is one next to St Mary's Church in Newport. It is only three feet high but has the inscribed cross and used to be on the Pilgrim path going out of Newport at Cnwc. Some people have suggested that the size of the circle is the accepted size of a loaf of bread provided to the pilgrims, a sort of medieval weights and measures symbol! This may be so but I think they also give a lot more information. They can be regarded as markers to show the path, give direction of travel and also where food and rest is to be had. For instance this stone has a line descending downwards to a circle with no cross. I think this can be interpreted as go back down the hill to find the major hostelry near Cwm and not at Nevern. Other stones show the cross at an angle which suggests that the vertical line is the main path direction. It was Pope Calixtus II in 1123 declared that two pilgrimages to St David's equalled one to Rome. Great numbers of pilgrims faithfully followed the well trodden path to the ecclesiastical capital of Wales.

In 1566 Newport was made up of twenty households, exactly the same number as Fishguard. St Dogmael's had twelve households but there were no households recorded at Solva. These figures do not make any sense and so I am assuming it is based on the houses or 'hearths' that paid tax at that time, not the number of Dwellings.

Cecil Nicholas who hailed from Dinas, was the Berthing Master at Fishguard Harbour when I worked there in the 1970's. While we waited for the Irish Ferries to arrive he passed on to me a lot of local maritime knowledge. Some of it he had remembered from when he was sitting on his grandmother's lap. He told me that when the sailing ships from Holyhead had cleared Bardsey they would sail due south until they saw Carningli. The peak of Carningli and the peaks of Mynydd Caregog/ Mynyddmelyn at Garn Fawr when seen 15 miles from the north make up two distinct humps. The sailors nicknamed these two humps on the horizon as the 'Dau Fron " or 'Two Breasts'. When I heard the story I did not take a lot of interest in it. However ten years later I was sailing that route and remembered his words.

Sure enough if you are looking for Fishguard from seaward there are no distinctive features on the coast to be seen from six miles away . You would think the high cliffs of Dinas head would be distinctive but the colour and shape of the entire coastline looks pretty much the same. I then looked for the two lumps or "breasts" above Dinas. Sure enough the old navigation marks could clearly be seen unchanged over the centuries. You aim for those and you come into the coast exactly where you want to be in Fishguard Bay. When I was involved with racing cruising yachts from Cardigan to Fishguard, I always won because I knew the tides. I knew when to hug the coast and when to sail out to catch the tide. This knowledge can only be gained from studying the tides on every trip. It cannot be gained from the Admiralty charts which often relate to tidal currents two miles out to sea and not the inshore waters. For instance most sailing boats leaving Cardigan had to leave on a high tide to get over the sand bar. If they wish to sail north they sail directly out to sea beyond Cardigan Island to gain the last two hours of the flood tide.

If you want to go West to Ireland or Fishguard you hug the coast at Cemaes Head away from the north going tide and only sail off the coast when the tide changes. It is a shame that such knowledge is getting lost through time. Today even sailing boats tend to rely on their engines to stem the tidal currents. But around the Pembrokeshire coast that is not possible with tidal currents of over 6 knots, navigation has to be done with the tides otherwise you get nowhere or you go backwards.

Even at the beginning of the 1900's it was not unusual to see thirty sailing vessels, mainly trading sloops, temporarily anchored in Newport Bay. Once goods started travelling by rail the sight of trading vessels under sail around the coast slowly diminished. The coastal vessels were sloops and schooners and those anchored in Newport Bay would be sailing in a northerly direction, waiting for the tide to change before sailing to New Quay and Aberystwyth. The vessels anchored in Fishguard Bay would be the coastal vessels going south or west. About to head off for Ireland or south to Milford Haven. They too would weigh anchor at High Water or one hour after so that by the time they get to Strumble Head they have seven hours of tide in their favour.

I regularly used to sail around Dinas Head. One day I was told "Never anchor off Dinas Head otherwise you will antagonize the pixies!" The notion of little people living under the sea there somewhat intrigued me. Sure enough, the legend states that a fisherman once anchored there and within a few minutes an angry sea elf had climbed up the warp and was gesticulating. "Do not anchor here again !" He shouted "your anchor has just gone through the roof of my house!" Anchoring around Dinas Head is not to be recommended anyway as the depths or substratum are not conducive to it. I then wondered if it was an amusing way of elders to pass on words of advice.

The Pembrokeshire Coast National Park path starts at St Dogmael's on the banks of the Teifi where some of the vessels owned by Newport traders were built. There you will see a wood sculpture of a mermaid, here is her story….

One day a fisherman named Peregrin was out in the bay off Poppit. Seeing something splashing in his net he suddenly realized he had caught a mermaid. Much to the consternation of the mermaid he hauled her into his boat. "Let me go, Let me go " pleaded the mermaid. But Peregrin had other ideas, especially as he had never caught a mermaid before. Eventually a deal was struck, the mermaid promised to give Peregrin three warning shouts in his time of greatest need. He let her go and with nothing to show the others what he had caught that day, he sadly returned home. A few weeks went by and he had not seen anything of his friend, but nobody else had seen her either. It was a flat calm sea and he was out in his boat again. Suddenly a voice shouts to him. "Peregrin, Peregrin, Peregrin !" It was the mermaid in the water behind him "Get In your nets, Get in your nets, a storm is coming!" Although the weather looked good, he knew that it was her warning so he pulled in his nets and rowed back into the estuary, telling others to do likewise. Within an hour a ferocious northerly hit the coast. Peregrin was saved but 27 fishermen who did not heed the mermaid's advice, were lost.

The mermaid story relates to a storm in September 1789. This is an original etching showing a peaceful scene outside Cemaes Head at about the same time. When you pass St Dogmael's look out for the mermaid, she is sitting at the top of the slipway waiting to give you some sound advice.

**Bedd yr Afanc**
(51.977384N :
4.756329W)

To find out the legends associated with this double line of stones you will need to visit the Internet. Here is a photo of myself myth-busting. The truth is even more unbelievable. It is in fact Britain's first aerodrome. Not for aircraft but for swans! The Neolithic believed in a Cycle of Life. Ashes in the Underworld developed into tadpoles. Frogs changed into birds. On death the birds took the souls to the Cygnus Star in the heavens. Later a swan falls to the ground bringing the souls back to earth, just like the stork bringing babies into the world. The ancestor is reborn. This line of stones is a marker to attract winter visiting swans to descend onto Brynberian moor. It lies in a half circle of ditches with a pond to one side. The stones are small for two reasons. To not hinder swans landing or on their runway when taking off. Also to help frogs get off the ground and fly into the heavens the stones are angled and only 0.5 m high. Frogs only need to be one foot off the ground to be able to take off to the Cygnus star. It is the same animal ritual area as Gors Fawr, a structure to attract frogs. This one is for both swans and frogs. I do not like dispelling good stories of a Welsh Loch Ness monster, but being a non-fiction author, I think the truth is equally as interesting. For more on the purpose of Pembrokeshire ancient stones see my latest book **Neolithic Pembrokeshire, Death, Dolmens, Frogs and Wisdom.**

## Newport's First School and Teacher Training College.

Madam Bevan (1698-1779) lived at Laugharne and was a great philanthropist and educationist. She never had any children but had the vision of having schools in every town in Wales. She, like the Bowens was related to the Phillips of Picton Castle. In about 1830 it was Bowen's money that commenced a school in Newport. The school at College Square was sometimes referred to as Madam Bevan's School of Navigation. Both adults and children attended and this grand title, infers that navigation was also taught. By calling it a 'School of Navigation', may have boosted the attendance levels, as all Newport boys aspired to be Master Mariners. This brings me on to mentioning the 'Welsh Not'. The movement afoot from 1840 to discourage Welsh being spoken in schools. Contrary to general belief it was not implemented by the Government as the Education Acts did not come into effect until the 1870's. Curiously it was first adopted by Welsh speaking teachers who must have seen it as a way to teach English in schools. The School in Lower St Mary Street (later the Youth Hostel and the West Wales Eco Centre) was built in 1874.

## The Wells

Before the introduction of a mains water supply in about the 1930's the townspeople relied on half a dozen wells situated around the town. It was the children's job to collect the water in two gallon cans (7.5 litres weighing 7.5 Kg) . The older folk explained what they used to do in the 1920's.

"On Mondays we used to carry water and it was heavy going! There were several wells in Newport." The old village pump was situated at the bottom of Lower St Mary's Street. The one we used to go to was the one at the Felin, the old mill" The children realized it was easier to walk downhill carrying the water than going uphill, even if it was a longer distance. " We could get drinking water from under Henrietta Mair's Bridge. Sometimes that dried up and we'd go up to Ffynnon Dreiag on the way up to Castle Hill. There was always water opposite Cottham Lodge. This well was destroyed by the side road being widened in about 2009. There was also a town well at Bentinck, and a place further up by Greystones."

"The well down in Long Street and the one down in Pen Bont, were tidal. You couldn't get water when the tide was in.
The tide had to go out for the spring to throw up lots of fresh water, otherwise it was covered."

## Holy Wells

Newport has a few Holy Wells, some of the over 240 that used to be known in Pembrokeshire alone. We are not talking about drinking wells of which there are thousands but wells associated with spiritual healing or having significant properties. In the winter months when the weather was not conducive to going diving I used to travel around Pembrokeshire studying these Holy Wells. One which was difficult to locate 50 years ago is now lost in a bramble bush and long forgotten. It was near the stepping stones at the bridge. Situated in the ground near the waterworks between the iron bridge and the Dental Practise. I see that Dyfed Archaeological Trust did a desk top study of them in 2011. The one most commonly quoted for Newport is half way up the northern slope of Carningli, in a cluster of rocks called Carn Cwn. Cups are carved out of the rock and it is a Wishing and a Curing Well of unknown date. Like two other wells in Newport the water flow is said to alter with the flood and ebb of the tide in Newport estuary.

Most of these ancient Wells have a tradition of bent pins being thrown in. The well in the Gwaun Valley near the churchyard in Llanllawer, (51:59.2070N 4:55.9807W) was even said to receive straight and bent pins on whether the wish was good or evil.
This Llanllawer well, was both a Curing well and a Cursing well. A cursing well is also found in Isles of Scilly. Cruelly bent pins were daily thrown into St. Warna's Well, Isle of Scilly to wish for ship wrecks! As the Llanllawer well also had a reputation for curing sore eyes, an offering was often given. One cannot receive without also giving. Theorists believe that a pin being something forged in metal, a mystical art driven by some super being, is why the pin was chosen. Most wishing wells were given one or two bent pins on the baptism of a child or to appease the Gods on Holy Days.

**Fynnon and Pystyll**

In Welsh there are two words that describe a well or spring. Ffynnon means a spring with bubbles in it, or a fountain. Pystyll is running water (no bubbles) more like a waterfall. Off big beach, Traethmawr, along the way to Pen Morfa is a waterfall call Pen Pistyll. In times of old the sailing ships when anchored in the bay would send a small boat out to the small beach below Pen Pystyll. Here, the sailors could have a fresh water shower and then fill a small barrel, canvas bucket or earthenware jug with fresh water for their daily needs.

*Lower reaches of the River Nevern before the Sand Bar.*

Many have the misunderstanding that shipwrecks happened because of a lack of proper charts. Some maybe, but our Newport ships would not not need charts. The boys manning the sloops would understand the voyages while undergoing their apprenticeships. They were being taught the routes through constantly sailing to the same ports with older folk who knew how to get there. These Victorian sailors knew more about the tides and weather forecasting that we give them credit for. The advances in weather forecasting has helped reduce ships being lost not the advancement in navigation. Modern ships rely too much on their fancy electronic equipment. More common sense and basic seamanship would result in less ships being lost in modern times; American Navy please note!

*A typical Ketch rig.* The type of vessel built around the Welsh coast around 1860's  If the masts were a similar height it would be classified as a Schooner. Before 1830's Newport built its ships from Baltic timber. After 1850's Cardigan ships were often built of timber from Nova Scotia.

When Newport School, Ysgol Bro Ingli was about to be built Dyfed Archaeological Trust spent a few months doing an archaeological survey of the site. I was fascinated at what they discovered. National Library Archives have a medieval map showing this area at the bottom of Long Street. It is the oldest town map existing in Wales. It delineates the burgesses houses and the names of those living in them, probably 90 years before the Castle was built. The wooden foundations of two timber houses were discovered and a pit nearby probably used for the curing of skins. It was thought these houses were abandoned in favour of stone built ones nearer the castle that was built about 1255. I am disheartened that I have failed to find any written report, even unpublished, of this excavation. There is little point in any Archeological exercise when the findings are unavailable or so difficult to find. Today even a ten minute You Tube video would suffice for the general public on what Dyfed Archaeological Trust has found out about Newport's medieval houses. A friend of mine from Goodwick bought a plot of land in Lower St Mary Street and was highly confused when he was required to pay a extra fee to obtain planning permission for a new build dwelling. The fee was to go to Dyfed Archaeological Trust to do a quick assessment of the land before foundations could be done. It is an excellent idea but if you are unaware of the reason and of what the Trust has found only 250 meters away it is somewhat baffling. I know of Newport long time residents who are completely unaware that a detailed dig was ever carried out in Long Street.

**Medieval kiln**
At least the people of Newport are now aware of the existence of the Medieval Kiln that was covered by the stage when the Memorial Hall was built in 1921. This 15th century kiln is the most complete of its kind in the UK. We must thank the builders of the Hall for their foresight in building the stage over this kiln that completely preserved the state of the kiln from 1922 to 2015. The Kiln is one of two on the site and was not just some local cottage industry but could fire 1,300 pots on one firing.

**Newport a hotbed of Alternative Ideas, Eco friendly houses, Green Living, Solar Power, Composting, Electric Bicycles, Vegan lifestyles and much more.**

Although the The Centre for Alternative Technology (CAT) located in the heart of mid Wales had already started in 1973, the West Wales Eco Centre was not far behind. Converting the Newport School building into an Information Office to advice on everything from Eco Tourism, Green friendly houses, vegetarian dishes to Council Grants on insulation. Everything to get people more aware of sustainability. It was the enthusiasm of Brian John, the local architects and many other practitioners that got Newport's West Wales Eco Centre started. Newport knows a lot about sustainability. During the 197O's the town was full of real and dreaming downshifters, some were seeking the whereabouts of the communal farm run by John Seymour. He had written books on Self Sufficiency. The success of his books was due to the timing of the publication and the wonderful illustrations by Sally, his wife. Vegan pilgrims would be wanting to know how to find the road to John Seymour's Fachongle Isaf, a 5 acre farm. How he managed to obtain such free labour for his smallholding was most amazing....I think the Carningli magic mushrooms must have helped in the recruitment!
I am glad to see that after more than 20 years of battling with National Parks that Brithdir Mawr and their unconventional houses and communal ways of life have finally obtained their planning permission.
Brian John wrote in 2016. "SOLAR ANNIVERSARY! We now have over 10,000 MW of installed solar PV capacity in the UK. Do you know where it all started? In Newport. Exactly 20 years ago, in Sept 1996, our West Wales Eco Centre started sending solar electricity into the grid. It was the UK pioneer. It was quite a battle, but we helped to write the rules (TAN8) that have regulated PV installations ever since. That was a little piece of history, and something for Newport to be proud of!"

**Twinning Of Towns.**

The twinning of Newport town with Annapolis was a bit of a mistake. When it happened Glyn Rees was Mayor and it was generally thought that he and his wife Penny, wanted a bit of a banquet and a USA holiday. Glyn and Penny Rees were social animals that ran the Golden Lion, which, incidentally, used to be called the Green Dragon before 1820. Consequently, without mentioning it to the rest of the town, Glyn twinned Newport with an American State City, 38 times larger than Newport. The following year distinguished members of Annapolis came to Newport to see the town they were officially twinned with. They were both horrified and amused. They thought they were twinning with Newport, Gwent, a more appropriate place with 150,000 inhabitants. Annapolis, state city of Maryland with Naval Academy has a population of 38,000. Nevertheless, the twinning has remained and much friendship has ensued.

Newport is also twinned with a coastal town of Plouguin in Brittany. I was on the Twinning Committee in 1993 and was forced by my wife and others to learn some Welsh and Breton before our first twinning visit.

Amongst the Newport contingent was Brian and Inger John and the larger than life figure of Newport's outstanding Town Crier. With his newly acquired tunic, specially designed using the red, white and black of the Ancient Borough's Coat of Arms he was undoubtedly the 'Man of the Match'. His name was Rob Roughley. He was a mountain of a man with a huge white beard and a voice to match. We all remembered how he both frightened and delighted the Brittany school kids who thought they had seen Santa Claus for the first time. He was a great asset to the town but unfortunately was not in good health and died soon after.

## Town Crier

As Newport has a Royal Decree to appoint its own Mayor, so too it can officially appoint its own Town Crier. This requires someone with a formidable presence and a commanding voice.

In 2016 Newport held a meeting of Town Criers who came from far and wide to show off their costumes and presence. Although regarded by some as a 'Bit of Nonsense' it nevertheless is an immensely important part of Newport's heritage and is to be encouraged and supported. Following photograph taken from www.facebook.com/NewportTownCrier

This picture shows the incumbent Town Crier, Michael Mathias brandishing his bell and strutting as beholds his position.

**Unaccompanied Singing**
We were to discover on our Twinning visits that unaccompanied singing is considered an important cultural Welsh /Breton thing. Today when our Breton cousins come to Newport, they bring a choir with them!. Amongst the memories of the older folk, was one that mentioned unaccompanied singing being taught in the Old School, now the Youth Hostel in town. "They altered the school in 1914, before that it was totally different. There was the Big Room and then there was the Babies Class. We used to have sewing and music. In the Babies Class we learnt to tie up boots, we had two strips of leather to learn on. And working with sand, making patterns. The desks were all facing the front, the fire was in the front. The heat from the coal fire didn't reach the back of the class. It was pretty cold at the back! We used to have some good concerts, singing and reciting, and little sketches, but no instruments." This last comment of no instruments struck a chord. I had come across a newspaper report of the Courte Leet in 1906. Prior to 1906 someone had donated instruments to the town to form a band but it never got going or the band was disbanded. At the meeting the Mayor was asked to recover the instruments so they could be given to the school. The Mayor failed to recover the musical instruments and certainly for the next decade there were no instruments at the school. There was a small Victorian piano at the school an important ingredient to give the right note to commence the unaccompanied singing.

**May Day**

One custom that seemed to die out around WWII days was the celebration of May Day. "Each little district used to have its own May Queen. And they would be dressed up …..We used to gather primroses and wild flowers and make little bunches, and pin them on the childrens' dresses. And we'd go round, a lot of us together, singing  Queen of May, Happy Day, This is the Way, To Play Queen of May ! And people would come out, and give up halfpennies."

## Court Leet

*Reported in the County Echo of 7th July 1910* The ancient corporation held a meeting at Lwyngwair Arms Hotel. The following Aldermen and Burgesses were sworn in as jury. John Williams, chemist. John Williams, draper. Dr.David Havard, J.P. Rev. George Morgan, John Hughes, Captain D. Mathias, HR Felix and D.Jones. Messrs GB Bowen (Llwyngwair) John Davies, David Evans, William Brown, John Rowe, John Ellis, David Lewis, David Thomas, and J Evans. They appointed Captain John Davies of Fern Cottage as Deputy Mayor and Mr J.B. Bowen, a Burgess. Amongst the agenda for this meeting was the concern that George Beer (of Sandy Haven) was taking sand from the beach. The question of erosion of the quay walls was discussed and if permission was to be granted who should any royalty go to?

Havard stated that he, as landowner, had maintained the quay wall near his property. I surmise this to be near the old saw pit not far from the Boat Club. Each Year the town is entitled to choose a Mayor and each year there is a ceremony of "Beating the Bounds" walking the boundary of the ancient Borough.

## Boy Scouts

J.B Bowen of Llwyngwair had the nickname "Van" and was a patron for starting the Boy Scouts into Newport in 1910. At the time Goodwick had the longest established Boy Scout group with four patrols named ***Lions, Kangaroos, Cuckoos and Hounds***. There was great rivalry between these scouts and the three patrols of Fishguard named ***Peewits, Foxes and Otters.*** The daughter at Llwyngwair use to be Master of the Boy Scouts. Each Saturday she would lay a trial of signs throughout the woods "She would have gone around Nevern, then, with all the signs. And we had to follow them, then. And we'd come back to the house (mansion) and have a big tea in the garden. We'd had a fire, and make our own tea, with our tins!" With inter Scout competitions one of the big events was the under 13 age boys 'Tug of War'.

## The Coastline.

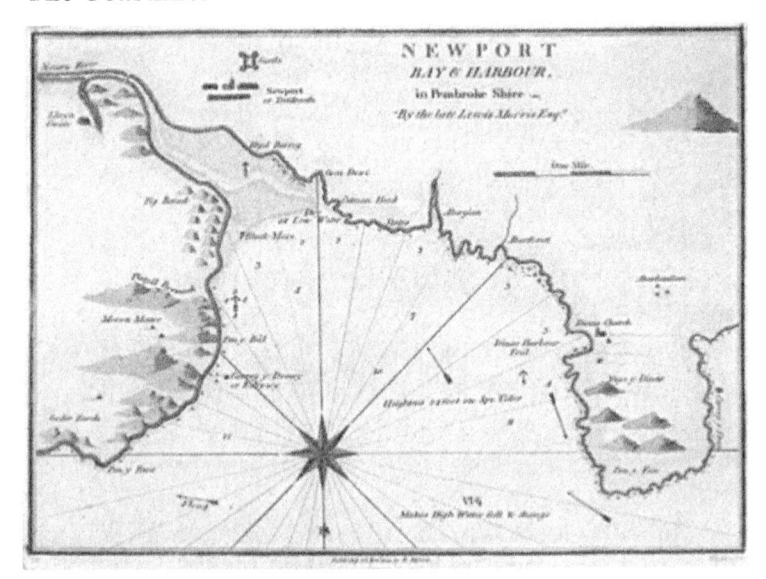

Lewis Morris was the first to produce sea charts of the harbours around Wales. The above is a chart drawn by his son William and was printed in 1800. It was recommended in about 1748 that two piers made from timber and stone be constructed just inside Newport sand bar to aid the unloading of ships and to allow the river to scour a deeper channel into the estuary. I cannot see that the suggestion would have accomplished such advantages. Perhaps that is why these so called harbour improvements were never carried out.

Before the days of GPS and before the days of yellow metric charts, the Admiralty produced black and white fathom charts. Surrounding the edges of the older charts were distinctive silhouettes of the coastline from certain angles. Any navigator will know that these were equally as important as the depths and the nature of the seabed. I was once told that the only difference between a map and a chart is that the latter has depth marks on it.

## River Nevern (Afon Nyfer)

The river is tidal as far as Llwyngwair Manor, and still navigable by kayak to a bridge in its grounds. I once read (unfortunately not making a reference) that one of the Welsh Princes or Princesses had a crown embedded with pearls that came from the *freshwater* pearl mussel, *(Margaritifera margaritifera)* from Nevern river.

Enquiries with the keeper of the Crown Jewels, Tower of London say they have no crowns or coronets known to have Nevern pearls. There is, however, a 1911 coronet that does contain pearls held by the National Museum of Wales but I have not contacted them about it. Undaunted I spent a long time in 1996 searching the river for any such mussel. After much investigation I did find three specimens in the highest reaches of Afon Bryn Berian. They are one of the favourite foods of the Otter *(Lutra lutra)*. Otter populations are now on the increase and I surmise that the freshwater mussel is now extinct throughout this river, vanishing only in the last twenty years.

In the sixteenth century when the town was developing, a stone bridge with six arches spanned the River Nevern. It existed in 1596 but was said to be demolished on purpose to stop the yellow plague from passing from Berry Hill side of the river to the town. This word yellow plague is a bit strange and I think probably means Bubonic plague where some of the coastal ports, such as Dale, lost 30%' of their population in the 17th century. The stepping stones were said to have been placed there then. Looking at the stepping stones just upstream of the Iron Bridge one would assume these were there in Pilgrims days four hundred years before any bridge was built. However we should heed what historians tell us and regard the stepping stones as an interim measure between the old stone bridge and the new Iron Bridge.

## Sewin and Salmon

Nevern is still an important trout, sewin and salmon river I was fortunate once to walk the river with an old man who had spent a lifetime as a poacher and gamekeeper. He showed me all the spots along the river, where you could lie down on the bank and put your arm under a tree root to tickle salmon. I even tried it once but I was not fast enough at throwing the fish onto the bank! Some of my acquaintances used to put illegal nets across the river but in my defence I was also responsible for proof reading the Sea Fisheries Byelaws banning the practice. One well known character who lived in a Council House in the middle of the town could never have a bath in his own house. Why ? Because it was always full of water and fresh salmon!

Fly Fishing for sewin at dusk on the middle stretches of the Nevern is one of the best river fishing experiences Wales can offer. I know of people who have come to live in North Pembrokeshire just to enjoy such occasions.

Sewin caught by fly fishing on River Nevern 2012.
*Photograph courtesy Nevern Angling Associaton .*

## Bowens of Llwyngwair

As a precis of Newport history we move from Welsh Princes at Nevern Castle to Norman Knights at Newport Castle . A family named Cole came from France with Martin de Tours, with William The Conqueror, from whom they received the grant of land. It would be nice to associate this Cole as a descendent of the French legendary figure "Old King Cole, a merry old soul etc. He was a keen agriculturalists and it is said with an auger from France, Cole studied the soils of the lands all the way down the west coast of Wales. Favourably impressed with the marl he found around Newport he chose his land at Llwyngwair. In 1326, William Cole was on a jury in Newport so we know he was living at Llwyngwair at that time. Sir James Bowen, adherent of Henry VII, bought the property from the Coles in 1503. Prior to that the family were living at Pentre Ifan. A timber vaulted roof structure still exists from the sixteenth century at Pentre Ifan.. James Bowen (the second) had no less than seventeen children, his eighth son emigrating to Boston, Massachusetts in 1640. For generations the Bowens of Llwyngwair were the feudal, 'Lord of the Manor', owning the farms and the mill adjoining. Great respect was given by the inhabitants of Newport to the Bowen's but it must be remembered that many of them were in their direct employ. What is not generally acknowledged is the enormous amount of landscaping that went on when the Manor was being built. Today as you approach there is a hump in the ground half way between the Lodge and the Mansion. This is a "Ha Ha"of sorts. It was built to hide the view of those in the Mansion from seeing the general public as they passed along the Cardigan road. It would have been constructed without mechanical labour and is a considerable amount of soil to move using a horse and cart and shovels.

All the woods and grounds around Llwyngwair were carefully designed and planted. Behind the mansion was an area made into a duck decoy, encouraging wild duck into a specific pond. Hazel trees were planted to encourage woodcock and on the map we can see a Cockshut Wood. A line of Sweet Chestnuts was planted on the high ground. Not only do these trees provide chestnuts to be roasted on the fire at Christmas but posts made from the branches do not rot in the ground.
The Hazel woods were coppiced for firewood and certain oaks pollarded to provide grown knees for the shipbuilding. The sandy lane between the Mansion and Nevern Church was brushed clear of leaves every Sunday to allow the Bowens to go to Nevern Church by horse and trap.
All the others working at the Mansion had to walk down the lane to Church, stopping to bow or courtesy and much doffing of hats as the Bowen's trap passed by.

The Bowens were sympathetic to the Methodist movement. Between 1772 and 1777 it is known that John Wesley stayed at Llwyngwair Mansion seven times. A large tree in the grounds where he preached still exists. The Bowens in the nineteenth century, and the Lloyds of Coedmor still spoke Welsh. They understood the importance of not dispelling the Welsh language. Llwyngwair translates as a 'bundle of hay' or a 'grove of grass'. On the biggest tides the sea water reaches the grounds of Llwyngwair. In doing so it passes Y Felin, the mill that ground all the corn. Small ships could load here and wheat was once an important export of Newport. The other notable export was Wool.
This early sea trading set the scene for Newport's maritime heritage. For the next 300 years similar trading was carried out on Newport ships sailing to Ireland, Bristol and North Wales.

**Essex Robert John Havard** was born on 16 June 1918. He was both a Town Councillor and a County Councillor. His family had run the ironmongers shop for at least three Generations. When he was interviewed by the school children he related two incidents concerning his family. " We used to do some very naughty things in those days! (referring to the 1920's). An uncle of mine and his friend got hold of some gunpowder that my Grandfather used to sell for the quarry. There were two old ladies sitting round the fire having a nice gossip and putting their feet up. The boys came inside the house quietly and threw some gun-powder on the fire. There was a terrible BANG and two terrific screeches! Legs in the air and skirts flying! At about the same time, Uncle Essex, my namesake, blew Newport School up! He was about ten or eleven. It was an abortive thing really, but the intention was there! They put the gunpowder under a stone, it was lucky they did not lose their eyesight!"

Essex would enjoy relating a tale of skirts flying and it reminded me of an incident in his shop about 1980. The goods in the shop were stacked in what appeared to be completely random order with no floor space to walk around. Some articles even marked up in shillings and pence that should have been abandoned a decade before. A visitor came into his shop and was bending over looking at something at floor level. Mrs Joan Harries who worked in the shop thought she recognised the woman as a regular customer. As a prank she grabbed the woman's private parts from behind. It was Joan Harries who got a shock when the woman turned around and it was someone she had never seen before. What I thought was so funny was that the visitor probably assumed it was Essex who was the culprit as he was standing next to both of them! They all had some explaining to do but it was all amicably sorted. The residents of the town soon heard about it and were highly amused, but also nodded and all agreed it was a typical story of the Havard family.

Since Levi Havard moved to Newport from Milford around 1760 the family ran the the biggest ironmongery store in town. This acted as a ship's chandler, general store and ironmongers. It supplied cord, anchors, cooking utensils and hardware to the ships, many of which were owned by the same Family. In the last ten years it is now run by a Scotsman, with the Havard name still proudly retained. The Havards imported the coal and delivered it to the hearths of the wealthy in the town. When a ship was built, launched and sold, it had to be complete and ready for sea. Not only was it fully rigged with sails from the Fishguard sailmaker already bent onto the yards but the ship's galley had to have a frying pan as well. All was arranged by the Havards. The Havard family have also been eminent in medicine. In 1894 the General Practitioner for Dinas to Cardigan was a Doctor Havard. John Havard was secretary of the British Medical Association from 1980 to 1989. In 1830 of the traders and merchants, David Havard, druggist, and stamp distributor and Levi Havard - shopkeeper and shipwright are mentioned.

Today the only boats sold at Havard's shop, now owned by a Scotsman, are kayaks and colourful blow up dinghies seen hanging up in East Street. The Havards stopped building ships in Newport around 1855.

When I was living in Newport in the 1980's I got to know Essex Havard well. He was such a gentle character that you couldn't miss him or not be familiar with his idiosyncrasies. I happened to see him the day the postman had delivered a letter to his house. Essex asked me if it was a joke and if I knew anything about it, half accusing me of its origin. I looked at the letter and studied the envelope and said it was no joke. It was definitely an invitation from Buckingham Palace for him to meet the Queen. He was being awarded for his outstanding services to Surf Lifesaving. He was a founder and father figure of the Newport Surf Lifesaving Club and had took the professional Surf Lifesaving exam to become Britain's oldest fully qualified beach lifeguard. He was 68 years old.

Essex used to run up the mountain road behind his house every morning with is young sheepdog trotting beside him. Not only that but (about 6 days a week), winter and summer, he went for a daily swim on Newport Beach. Essex lived in a large terrace house on the Mount. On the corner to the mountain road opposite is where the town gallows used to be. When it was last used I do not know, probably around 1770, the cemetery is just up the road.

**Newport Surf Lifesaving Club**
The Club commenced about 1971 and soon had their own Inshore Lifeboat. It was at a time when the RNLI were starting to initiate Inshore Rescue stations around the coast. Together with a group of Coastguards, John Pattinson and myself attended a week's training course at Aberavon with Commander Thomson. It was a Coxswain Training Course for Inshore Lifeboats and showed us how to launch inflatable craft from a beach directly into the surf.
The Surf Lifeaving Club was small in numbers and in the 1980's had difficulty in finding enough people to form a team for the annual competitions. On one occasion to make up numbers in a Lifeguard Competition, the Newport team invited the swimming teacher from Fishguard to join them. He eagerly accepted the challenge as he considered himself a strong swimmer and lifesaver. However he was not accustomed to cold sea water swims and failed to perform when needed. Essex, on the other hand, twice his age could sea swim twice as fast and twice as far. It confirms my belief that beach lifeguards have to train in the sea and not in a heated indoor pool..

*Photograph of Essex* in super-man pose for the local newspaper. He was the Guardian of the beach and the town and got a medal from the Queen to prove it!

**Newport's earliest known ship.**

One of the earliest records of a Newport vessel is in 1566. Owen Picton was the owner of a 6 ton vessel called **Le Savoir,** (spelt Savyour). The ship was probably built locally. Owen Picton was one of the leading gentry tradesman living in St Mary's Street, and was the leading Merchant of Newport in 1566- 1567. He owned the only ship recorded as trading out of Newport in the medieval Welsh Port Books. On 18 July 1566 the vessel **'Le Saviour'** of Newport sailed to Bristol under Captain John Roberts, with a crew of three. The cargo was cloth and slates, comprising 1 pack of fardel [bundle] of frieses [coarse woollen cloth with a nap on one side] and 11,000 slate Stones. On 16th August the same vessel sailed from Bristol to Newport, under Captain Henry Roberts, with iron, tar, pitch, alum, white salt, soap, linen etc. On 12 September 1567 it sailed (under Henry Roberts) with a similar cargo; and on 31 July 1567 it sailed (again under Captain Henry Roberts) with six tons of coal - the merchant in each case being Owen Picton of Newport, who "useth commonly to trade to Ireland, North Wales and up Severne afishinge" The grandson of this merchant was Owain Picton who lived at the manor house of Trellyfaint. It is noted that the Pictons, and the Philipps of Picton Castle are related in marriage to the Bowens of Llwyngwair. Descendants of John and Henry Roberts who Captained the ship for Owain (Owen) Picton are undoubtedly the same Roberts family that own Castle Farm and Llwyngwair Farm today.

George Owen of Henllys, the great Victorian writer of the area was a descendent of Owain Picton, and his father and father before him both Lords of Cemaes.

Newport's geographical position in St George's Channel made it a convenient base for its sloops to trade with the Irish ports of Wexford and Waterford and also the North Wales ports and south eastward to Milford Haven and Swansea.

Geraint J.Jenkins wrote a book Maritime Heritage of Ceredigion, including something of the ships built at Cardigan and in the Teifi Estuary. Although perhaps outside the remit of the book, it was disappointing to see that there was almost no mention of shipbuilding at Newport, only ten miles to the south. Newport's maritime history is an integral part of Teifi heritage. In fact the number of ships built at Newport was at least half the number constructed on the River Teifi. Curiously there seems to have been little animosity between St Dogmaels folk and those of Newport. The families intermixed and there were owners and captains on both Cardigan and Newport built ships. All vessels built and working out of Newport, Fishguard and Cardigan were, prior to 1840, registered at the port of Cardigan. Later those based at Fishguard would be included in the Milford Registers. The Customs and Board of Trade ledgers for the port of Cardigan are still in existence, and the ship registers from 1827 are to be seen at the Pembrokeshire Archives office in Haverfordwest. I used to study these folders in the 1980's when they were at the Pembrokeshire Record's Office. These provide the basis of the information given here. While doing my research I met Leslie Owen (of Templeton) who was researching in detail the socio-economics of three of the schooners operating out of Newport. He died a year later and I know not if his study papers are still in existence. Hopefully his notes were deposited with the Pembrokeshire Record Office after his death. I often reflect on this, the fact that singularly someone can spend immense time and energy researching some obscure subject but if it is not put into print, on his death all that unique study is lost to the world. I still spend time researching wrecks, and I now find that some of the references I come across are from my own books written just 40 years ago. However, the information that I have put into print is only a fraction of the content that I actually possess.

An E. Kennion etching after Henry Gastineau (1791-1876) print about 1835 of Cwm yr Eglwys before St Brynach's church was washed away in 1859. The small vessel sailing out is a fishing boat with a Dandy rig commonly used on the West coast of Wales. I have only come across details of two Dinas built vessels. **John** a Sloop of 27 ton, built in 1828, named after her master and owner a John Lewis of Dinas. Another Sloop, also built at Dinas, one assumes at Cwm yr Eglwys, was the 37 ft long **Twins** in 1822. Another Sloop named **Dinas,** of 38 ton, had Newport and Dinas owners but was built at Abercastle in 1820. In the great gale of October 1859 the New Quay built Schooner **Mathildis,** with a cargo of culm, was wrecked to the east of Cwm yr Eglwys Church and all her crew of six drowned. She was 96 tons, built 1842 in New Quay and had dimensions 68 feet long x 18.5 feet beam x 10 feet. Draught  Official no. 13144. Joshua Jones her master was one of the six drowned. Another two smacks and their crew were also lost with the newspaper reporting the next day, "bodies floating everywhere". One of these was the **Swansea Trader** carrying roofing slates. In all eight bodies were recovered from the water and the cliffs and taken for burial.

**Shipwrecks.**

A storm of tremendous proportions hit the coasts of Wales, England and North of France on 13th January 1843. This "hurricane caused the loss of 180 ships and made 450 victims. No less than 22 vessels were wrecked or stranded along the shore of Cardigan Bay alone. A sloop of Aberayron broke away from her two anchors in St Tudwall's Road and was driven south by the gale. At about 5 am those on the sloop saw a schooner sinking close to the reef known as Sarn-y-Bwlch. They were in no condition to help and it was supposed all perished. Another vessel was seen in a sunken state north of Aberystwyth and a small boat with five men went out the next morning to see if they could find anyone alive. They too were lost and their bodies washed ashore. On the coast somewhere near Borth a small boat washed ashore that was marked ***David Havard, Phoebe. Newport.*** The boat was empty and no men were ever found. A report from Aberdovey a few days later confirmed that three schooners had been wrecked. One mast of the **Phoebe** of Cardigan still showing above the water three miles north of Aberdovey, all hands lost. Her master was David Havard (aged 41 years), the schooner named after his wife or mother. The crew lost probably numbered 5 other sailors from Newport. "On Friday last a severe gale of wind blew from the N.W. On the following morning the masts of a vessel were seen, about 3 miles to the north of Aberdovey Bar. The life-boat was immediately launched, and, commanded by Captains Timothy and Price, proceeded to the wreck, but there were no tidings of the crew. All must have perished. The vessel is called the **Phoebe,** of Newport, Port of Cardigan, 123 tons, Captain Havard, as appears by some old papers that came ashore from her ."(Newspaper article). Phoebe Havard was still alive living in Newport in 1854 but a widow. Another Phoebe Havard, aged 54, was living at the Eagle Inn, Cardigan at the time.

*The Illustrated Usk Observer and Raglan Herald   2nd March 1861.*

"During a fearful gale, at 6 a.m. on the 13th March 1861, the cable of a coasting sloop, the **Mary and Ann,** of Newport, Pembroke, snapped asunder, close under the cliffs, about half a mile below where the French invading force, under General Tate, landed on Pencaer, 67 years ago. Intelligence of the wreck was brought to the Fishguard Lifeboat Station, and the lifeboat was expeditiously manned and rowed round the coast to the spot. The sloop was wrecked against a small precipitous island, with a channel between it and the main land about 40 yards across, through which the sea burst with great fury. One of the crew of the sloop was cast by the waves on "the side of the cliff facing the land. Another could be seen lying on his stomach, with his head to windward, clinging to a ledge of rock seaward of the island, every wave washing over him. Several ladders were lashed together and a rope made fast to the top. This extempore bridge was thrown across the channel, but was immediately broken by the force of the waves, and the ladders and rope washed adrift. The lifeboat arrived, but from danger of being wrecked could not be of any service. Albert Furlong, aged 19, a native of Fishguard, then volunteered to swim across the channel with a rope tied to his waist, so as to be hauled back if unsuccessful; but the bystanders refused, judging by the fury of the waves and his apparent physical incapacity for such a feat that he would certainly be drowned. David Beddoe, a sea-man, nothing daunted by their refusal, slipped off his coat and waistcoat, climbed down the cliff, and plunged into the sea, closely followed by Furlong. The bystanders actually ran away "rather than see two men drown in that way."

After several times missing his hold of the opposite rocks, Beddoe got a footing, when at the end of the channel, and within a few feet of being washed out. to sea. Young Furlong, also, after frequently missing his hold, grasped some seaweed, and managed to get a footing beyond reach of the waves. Their late companions had by this time mustered curiosity to look after their fate, and seeing the heroes so far safe one ventured across with a rope and was pulled up by Beddoe and Furlong. It was a comparatively easy task to rescue the shipwrecked man on the land side of the island, but a work of great difficulty to climb down the seaward side of the cliff and save the one on the ledge of jock, who by this time, 2 p.m., must be benumbed. A stone was made fast to the end of a rope and thrown to him, and he had sufficient animation to make it fast around himself and was hauled to the summit of the island. They were all afterwards drawn to the main-land by ropes, it being 4 p.m, before the last man reached the mainland. One lad, aged 14, was washed away from the wreck and drowned. The man who had been on the ledge was about 60, and by the time he reached the mainland his arms were stiff in the position he grasped the rock, and he evidently could not have lived there much longer".

Although an extensive report on the rescue, I was a bit confused as to the identity of the ship and that she was anchoring in an unusual spot on the coast. The Pembrokeshire Herald and General Advertiser gave me the answers and her identity. The vessel was not the **Mary and Ann** a schooner, but the sloop **Elizabeth & Mary.** I had to find out if it was connected with Newport Pembrokeshire as the previous report had suggested.

According to Richard Larn Shipwreck Index Vol 5. the schooner was the 61 ton **Elizabeth and Mary**, built 1856 at Granton, Scotland and Registered at Limekilns. With an owner Mclaren. This is the only likely contender if you look in Lloyds 1859 registers . The Pembrokeshire newspaper reports ". The unfortunate men, it appears, with a boy, left Milford on the morning of Monday, in the smack **Elizabeth & Mary**,' for Newport, with a cargo of culm after arriving outside Fishguard harbour, and encountering a terrific gale, which split her foresail, she was compelled to put back to Carreg Owen Roads here she came to anchor, about six o'clock. However on the morning of Tuesday, during a frightful squall, her, chain parted and she was driven with great violence against the rocks at Carreg Owen." I call this rock Carreg Onnen and is the one immediately to the south west of Ynys Meicel the one that now has Strumble Lighthouse on it. " The old man and the boy first left the sinking vessel, the master (Jenkins) followed, and having as he considered helped the boy to a secure position on the rock, he endeavoured to provide for his own safety. A few moments afterwards, on looking round, he found to his horror that the boy had disappeared, a heavy sea had undoubtedly proved too much for his feeble strength at any rate he was gone and the waves danced wildly over the poor fellow's grave all hopes of rendering him any assistance was of course out of the question. The unfortunate lad was the son of Thomas Griffiths, the well- known ferry-man at Newport." The vessel had indeed a Newport connection although I knew the vessel was not the one built in Newport in 1792. Although Larn records her as this 61 ton schooner the papers all say a small sloop, which is implied by two men and a boy sailing her. I had to search for a sloop owned by Newport that was lost at this time.

Albert Furlong of Fishguard received three medals of bravery for saving two lives that day. One from the Royal Humane Society, one from the RNLI and one from the Shipwrecked Mariners Society.

It took me some time to realize that Larn in his entry for this shipwreck had done his own research and included the wrong vessel. He has looked in Lloyds register for **Elizabeth and Mary** for that date and seeing only two entries has erroneously picked one of them. Lloyds Registers has a 25 ton smack built in Wales in 1841, belonging to Barmouth named the **Elizabeth and Mary**. In 1846 she had master as Griffith and then a W.Owen added with Griffith as owners. We know that the boy lost was a Griffith so the links seems promising.

The papers say the captain's name was Jenkins, yet Larn has Mc Laren. I am beginning to see what is happening with the recording of this incident. By 1857 the vessel is not seen in Lloyds which is when her A1 classification would have expired. In 1843 Lloyds has a 38 ton smack of the same name built 1841 in Cardigan with J.Evans as master and Evans as owner. In 1844 Lloyds a different Barmouth registered smack named **Elizabeth and Mary** is recorded. 35 ton and Edwards master/owner.This was built at Lancaster (not Wales) in 1837. The Griffiths smack is not in Lloyds in 1844 which is very odd as she should still have her A1 rating. Although many of the vessels of less than 30 ton seem to drop out of Lloyds listing at this time. In 1855 she is not seen in Lloyds although a much larger 56 ton sloop registered in New Quay built in 1840 is listed with a T.Davies as master owner.

The Strumble Head smack lost is surely one of the above and I would guess it is the 25 ton smack the smallest of the Barmouth registered ones, built in Wales in 1841 and owned by Griffiths. Indeed it is quite possible that Thomas Griffith was his early master or owner before he moved to Newport to act as ferryman in his retirement.

As a follow up, it would be interesting if divers could look underwater at Carreg Onnen to see if there is anything left on the seabed of this Newport Smack. I have dived on the extremity of Ynys Onnen which drops off to 27 meters and have seen an anchor, but one considered earlier than 1800. I have never dived on the south or south east side of Carreg Onnen which is where the wreck would lie. In the 1970's a group of University divers asked me if there was any wreck that they could search for and survey. I suggested that they look for this wreck on the outer side of Carreg Onnen, adding that I knew of nobody who had dived there. They took up the offer and within two dives they had found wreckage and an anchor in a north west facing gully where I had directed them. They were so excited they rang me up and said they would show me the next day. I had to decline their offer as I was diving on a 'new' steamer wreck that I had recently discovered. Curiously, I never returned to the spot on Carreg Onnen, where they had seen wreckage. At that time I had not realized that the **Elizabeth and Mary** had anchored to shelter from the storm in the Roadstead and would have been wrecked on the inner side of the same rock. The group had found a wreck but a different one to the one I was expecting them to find.

I have been forced to use the same sheltering place in bad weather and found that the holding is not particularly good. Fishguard friends of mine brought a yacht round to Fishguard from Southampton and desperately wanted to sail the journey in one go without stopping. With adverse winds and tide at Strumble they were forced to spend a tide at this anchorage unable to weather the last few miles home. The holding ground is not that good and is best when the gap between the island and the lighthouse rock opens up. However your anchor is not likely to hold, especially in strong winds, like the captain of the **Elizabeth and Mary** found out to his peril.

This is a painting of a tranquil scene showing a sloop, already loaded, waiting for the tide to lift her off. It is all conjecture but if painted around 1861, it could be showing Thomas Griffiths (ferry man) rowing his wife, and another shareholder out to the **Elizabeth and Mary**, an hour before departure. Their dog is seen swimming behind. They had more than a vested interest in this 25 ton Smack, their 14 year old son was one of the three crew. They were seeing him off, and wishing him well. Their wishes were not enough for tragically their son was drowned when the smack was wrecked near Strumble Head. The painting has truly captured a scene of serenity and completeness, but it was a moment in time never to be repeated as this was the last time the **Elizabeth and Mary** was seen at Parrog.

This painting could be the **Elizabeth & Mary** about to depart on her last voyage in 1861. The tide is rising. On the extreme right bottom corner is a spaniel dog following the boat that has the owners wishing the crew a safe voyage.

**Loss of the Mary Ann.**
By having the advantage of reading old copies (from 1893) of the County Echo online, I was able to find what was happening to Samuel Griffiths and his mate the day the **Mary Ann** was wrecked. The smack had left Goodwick and was attempting to go south around Strumble Head. The smack was in ballast and would not sail correctly and ended up drifting ashore somewhere near Strumble Head. One of the Coastguard team helped the two men on board to get the vessel floating again, but in the act of sailing away the smack hit another rock which knocked her rudder off. In a leaking state and not being able to steer, Captain Griffiths took the vessel along the Pencaer coast towards Abermawr. Knowing the vessel was disabled and sinking the Coastguards near Strumble summoned the Rocket Brigade and the rowing Lifeboat at Goodwick to go to help the stricken smack. By the time the Rocket Brigade arrived the **Mary Ann** had anchored off Aberbach . Mrs Bowen Harries of Tresissillt could see the two men on the sinking ship and to let them know that help was arriving she made up a big sign on a blackboard "Lifeboat coming". She posted this on the cliff top where the distressed men could see it. The cliff rescue team actually fired their second rocket successfully over the gaff boom of the smack. Captain Griffiths did not like the idea of being hauled through the cold water with a breeches buoy and had other ideas. Unable to haul up the anchors, but knowing that the rescue team was there, he slipped the anchor cables and the smack slowly drifted ashore onto Abermawr beach. When the vessel stranded two of the rescue team waded out to the wreck taking with them cork lifejackets and brought the two weary men ashore. By the time the Lifeboat got to the scene the rescue was all over.
The Harries family from Tregwynt and Mrs Bowen Harries of Tresissillt, gave great hospitality and food to not only to the rescued but to the Cliff Rescue Brigade and the Lifeboat crew. Mr D. Bowen launched his own small boat from the beach and took food out to refresh the Lifeboat crew.

When they departed from the scene the smack was on her side in the surf and subsequent high tides smashed her hull to bits. . .
*Precis of County Echo article 17 May 1906.*
This sloop was built in Newport in 1816. The shipbuilder was William Lloyd, one of only two builders of ships on the banks of the River Nevern. The other builder was Levi Havard who, as we shall investigate, was the main shipbuilder, building at least 35 ships until his retirement around 1837. The **Mary Ann** was the second ship of that name. Six years earlier Lloyd had built a **Mary Ann** of similar dimensions that was lost in 1859. . Looking at all the ships built over the period 1760 to 1840 we see that both shipbuilders stuck to two types of vessel. It was either a large brig of 120 to 160 ton or a small sloop of 28 ton. In those days the families were often large ones with the sons learning the trade of mariner. When a Havard ship was built its building was often supervised by one of his sons who would then become master of that ship from its launch. He would have completed his seaman apprenticeship working on similar sloops for the previous five to seven years. By supervising the building of the ship, he would have intimate knowledge of its construction, a decided advantage when repairs were needed. He would also gain managerial qualities of working with older men, a necessary qualification for being an able captain. Once master of a sloop, he is likely to spend his whole career with that vessel. The vessel was likely to be named after his wife or his mother, thus we see a predominance of Victorian ladies names in the Custom's registers. Members of his family would be amongst the 64 shareholder owners of the vessel. In good trading times they benefited from profits and dividends. If the vessel was wrecked with a cargo, although some insurance may be had, it was a bitter blow to the family income and to the community. Imagine too, the devastation if the master and other family members were lost in
the same shipwreck.

It has been noted in this research that all the Havard ships were properly insured. This would not be the case with other Welsh owners who did not have the means to insure or would be prepared to take the risk of loss. To spread their losses, the families were large and wives or widows of the sea captains were shareholders on as many vessels as they could afford.
Understanding the interaction of the families, their reliance on their ships and trade give us an appreciation of how Newport developed in Victorian times.

**Lower Fishguard.** In 1790 Graeme Spence a master mariner proposed a pier at Fishguard extending 500 feet towards Goodwick from Castle Point locally known now as the Fort. His proposal to the Admiralty Commissioners was that it would provide a Harbour of Refuge for vessels that could not make it around the Smalls or St David's Head in storm conditions. He explained that 17 sailing vessels had been lost in the previous 20 years that otherwise may have been saved if they could have got to a place of shelter in Fishguard. His proposal would have meant even 14 foot draught vessel could enter the Lower Fishguard Harbour on High Tides. His idea was that a flag on the end of the pier, and a light at night would show when there was 12 feet of water inside. Such a scheme was also proposed by resident Harbour Master twenty years later but only the inner quays were constructed about 1830 and 1840 and this useful outer pier was never built. A stone built bridge with five arches was in existence in 1790, which can be seen in the early pre 1880 photographs of Abergwaun. What I was particularly interested in was his description of the tides at Fishguard. "On the full and change days of the moon it is High Water at 6.45 and Low Water a little after One. On the quarter days (ie Neaps) it is High Water on the shore at about a quarter after 12 and Low Water a little after 6." He continued to say that Spring range was 15 to 17 feet maximum and on Neaps about 4 to 6 feet. Thus no need for tidetables, just know the phases of the moon! The High Tide in Fishguard and Newport is one hour later

Being able to search through years of newspapers online I now find some Newport vessels that I never knew existed. For instance seen in *17th September 1869 The Pembrokeshire Herald and General Advertiser* ST. DAVID'S Yesterday (Sunday) morning, 'during a heavy gale the smack **Jane and Catherine,** of Newport, Pembrokeshire, came ashore in Ramsey Sound, and is a total wreck. Crew saved, almost miraculously. Thismorning the smack **Aid,** James, of the same port, is reported ashore. Crewsaved. No doubt the vessel will a complete wreck. The smack **Mary,** of Cardigan, a narrow escape, but she now rides pretty safely in the Island Roads."

These Island Roads refers to the anchorages within Ramsey Sound, a place that most would not expect to be a roadstead where ships would shelter. The area nearer to the landing spot at Ramsey used to be called the Waterings, one assumes because water could be obtained from the small stream. To understand more about the anchorage, I spent a night on a 34 foot yacht on anchor at this spot, only a hundred meters away from the Bitches. I must admit I was a bit concerned when, in the middle of the night, you can hear the tremendous roar of water cascading ferociously through these rocks, at speeds exceeding 7 knots. However as I knew there was always a back current close in to the island and that it was a traditional anchorage, my fear was somewhat alleviated. The anchor for the best part was never under strain. In fact most of the time the anchor cable lay slack. To the north of this is another waterfall that was used by the sailors to collect Ramsey Island water. It is near here my diving colleagues, Louise and Martin Coleman and Greg Evans discovered the wrecksite of what we think is the Newport smack David.

There are few things that could associate this wreck as a Havard built ship. A robust single prism glass deck fitting was found. I surmise that few sloops at the time would be built with such refinements but if we look on the **Artuose** accounts page, we can see that Havard paid seven shillings for one to put into a ship he was building in 1840. The Havards set the standards for wooden ship building in the 1820's to 1830's and putting an expensive glass natural light fitting into the deck of a small sloop like the **David**, would have been his style.

*Seen in the County Echo 25th October 1906*
**Wreck of the Anne of Newport**
CARDIGAN LIFEBOAT TO THE RESCUE. Captain David Luke, of Parrog, coal and culm merchant, has been unfortunate in losing the vessel he, the other day, purchased from North Wales. After making three journeys to Newport with coal and culm disaster befell her on the fourth and the **Anne** sank in deep water. Once again Captain Samuel Griffiths, Tyrhos, has had a narrow escape with his life for he had gone into his cabin thoroughly exhausted and was preparing to meet his Maker. The water in the cabin had reached the waists of the skipper and his mate and gloom s to be inevitable. The following was reported in the dailies ... On Sunday morning a sailing-ship drifted into Cardigan Bay, just outside the bar at Gwbert-on-the-Sea, having had her sails carried away on the previous night. At 10 o'clock the lifeboat crew were summoned by the firing of a rocket, and they assembled in a short time, and the boat proceeded to render what assistance could be given. It was blowing hard, and rain descended in torrents at the time. Before the lifeboat reached her she was some miles out at sea again, the wind having shifted. The vessel turned out to be the smack **Anne**,' of Newport, Pembrokeshire. After a chase of two hours under sail the lifeboat caught the **Anne** some 12 miles from land in a sinking condition, with the crew of two old men exhausted after having been at the pump since Saturday evening. Soon after the crew were transferred to the lifeboat the vessel sank, and the lifeboat returned to its station, in the teeth of an adverse wind about 6 p.m. The vessel had a cargo of culm for Newport, Pem., and had been showing signals of distress since an early hour on Saturday night at Strumble Head but these were not responded to until the vessel drifted before the wind and tide to Cardigan Bay. The lifeboat (which is a new one, and possesses the latest improvements) behaved splendidly, and worked its way back a distance of 12 miles against the wind. Captain Samuel Griffiths, had with him, as mate on this occasion, Mr VV Davies, of Church- street, who is over middle-age, not old as reported.

The vessel encountered bad weather and so became unseaworthy. Only the cargo was covered by insurance, the vessel itself being a Total Loss. Much disappointment is created in Newport because culm was especially ordered by many families for the winter. Further, the people were proud of the vessel being locally owned. Fuel is landed by vessel cheaper than by road vehicle, hence the keen regret at the wreck and the pecuniary loss Capt Luke has sustained. The disaster would seem to demonstrate that veteran Capt Samuel Griffiths bears a charmed immunity from harm by shipwreck. This is the second time he has been rescued from within a few months. The schooner **Mary Ann**, belonging to Capt Evans, Ship Inn, Newport, was distressed under Strumble Head, having lost her rudder and that she was run ashore at Abermawr, the Coastguards and rocket apparatus crew taking off Capt Griffiths and his mate. Subsequently the vessel broke up and Mr H.M.Harries, Tregwynt, purchased the timber for a few pounds.

It was the loss of the **Mary Ann** that determined Capt Luke in purchasing the **Anne** for local trade and, pluckily, the hardy veteran, son of sea, accompanied the purchaser to take charge of the craft. Although 75 years of age Capt Griffiths, despite his trying experiences and narrow escapes from almost certain death, cheerfully took command of the vessel, showing the hardiness and courage of Newportians and North Pembrokians generally at seafaring. To the aged skipper dry land is as trying and unnatural as it is to the denizens of the deep. In short he is a born sailor. There is something pathetic in his latest experience. The **Anne** had a heavy list, sails had been carried away and she was leaking badly. Both skipper and mate worked like Trojans at the pumps to keep the craft afloat. Probably the hazy weather of Saturday last obscured the signals of distress displayed on the **Anne** and on Sunday morning, it is stated, a steamer passed close by her way to Cardigan and reported passing a vessel flying distress signals. It is difficult to credit any vessel would pass another at the mercy of the sea in such a helpless state. However, the St.Dogmael's Lifeboat was got out and on reaching the craft found the captain and mate hard at work keeping the vessel afloat.

For some reason not quite clear, the Lifeboat was about to return without the skipper and mate.
Presumably Capt Griffiths was labouring under the impression that he could save the ship unaided, but finding the task an impossible one again re-called his rescuers. By this time the courageous pair had expended all their energy only to see their craft was doomed. They were now up to their waists in water which was fast gaining upon them, and it will been seen by the foregoing that the rescue was not a minute too soon. So exhausted was the aged mariner that he had no sooner been put into the lifeboat than he fell asleep like a weary, worn out voyager on the world's highway. After landing at St. Dogmael's the two were housed and hospitably treated. On Monday both the hardy shipwrecked fellows journeyed to Newport and by all appearances were little the worse, physically, for their trying experiences. Had the weather been less moderate probably neither would have survived to tell the tale. Much sympathy is felt for everyone concerned. It adds another page to the thrilling experiences of the venerable skipper who is a typical lion of the ocean.'

Newspapers rarely report a rescue in such graphic detail and we are fortunate that it relates to a Newport vessel with a local captain, just outside Newport Bay. A different report says that the two men had abandoned the distressed smack but their small boat had swamped in the big seas just as the Lifeboat arrived. The **Anne** was a 27 ton sloop recently bought by D.Luke of Newport. She was built in Conway in 1841 so the vessel was already 65 years old. In the previous months she had completed three culm trips. This was her fourth trip with culm cargo from Milford and was on her way to Newport when the incident occurred.
The other Newport vessel in the story is the 25 ton Smack **Mary Ann.** She was wrecked at Abermawr on 14th May 1906. ( See her story told elsewhere in this book).

The building of Fishguard Harbour at Goodwick in 1906 and the commencement of fast transport of goods and people brought big changes to trade and commerce for the area. Goods no longer needed an arduous sea journey from London to Newport. They could arrive from Paddington on the overnight train. Goods from Ireland could cross the Irish Sea in three and a half hours. Transatlantic ships were unloading their mail at Fishguard, as the train could then get the mail to London directly, while passengers had to disembark at Liverpool. In 1909 an article in the local newspaper the County Echo, compares the changes and reminds us of the emigration of passengers on the **Albion.**

" Newport (Pem.) as an Atlantic Port Ninety-one Years Ago. Nowhere, probably, has the adoption of Fishguard as an Atlantic port of call aroused greater interest or more enthusiasm than in the Ancient Borough of Newport (Pem.), where every other man whom one encounters is either a past, a present, or a potential mariner, and where captains' certificates are as prolific as the town's recent record apple harvest. Yet, how many of those who, reared in the picturesque old Borough, and earning their livelihood from the waters on whose marge she stands, are aware that she was an Atlantic port ere e'er Fishguard was dreamed of as aught but an agricultural and fishing centre ? Yet, such is undoubtedly the case The Liverpool Daily Post and Mercury has recently unearthed an interesting old record, printed in Welsh, giving an account I of the voyage of the brig **Albion,** with passengers and emigrants, from Caernarvon, North Wales, to North America, in the year 1818, and by way of showing the contrast in the experiences of ocean travellers, gives a few extracts therefrom.

The record appears to have been written daily by the captain, Llewelyn Davies, of Cardigan, who was in charge of the ship,' which was purchased by a wealthy local magnate of Carnarvonshire, Mr Griffith Jones, of Talysarn, for the purpose of transporting a large number of families and others from his county who desired to seek their fortunes in America. After some days of preparation and provisioning, the vessel was moored in the Menai Straits on the 18th May, the next day being wholly occupied in getting all the passengers, with their luggage, on board. On the 20th the King's officers made a minute inspection of all, and saw that every passenger was provided with sufficient food for three months. On the 21st the pilot came on board, and with very mixed feelings the voyagers passed out of sight of the ancient walls of Caernarvon, most of them never to see that famous old place again. The first night at sea was spent at anchor near the coast, and, after the pilot and owner had left, the passage was resumed in a fair wind. Seven heads of families were chosen to form a committee for the purpose of drawing up a code of rules to be observed by all passengers during the voyage. The first rule provided for the proper observance of the Sabbath, when all were to attend Divine service, decently dressed, punctually at 10 a.m. The second rule was to prohibit swearing and the use of bad language, and whoever offended in this was to be put on half the allowance of water and compelled to wear a badge. Stealing was prohibited by the third rule, and anyone found guilty of this had to clean the lower deck for a whole week, and to wear a certain distinctive badge. Anyone found guilty of telling lies was sentenced to undergo, a much more nauseating task; and there were several other rules as to general behaviour, with varying punishments, from being put last in rotation to cook their meals to the more rigid one of being put in the stocks.

Having dropped anchor near Newport, Pembrokeshire, the captain went ashore to see his family, and some of the passengers also went ashore by the same boat to purchase certain necessaries they had forgotten. The vessel and its passengers attracted considerable curiosity among those on shore, for it was then a very rare sight to see a load of Welsh passengers leaving their country to seek their fortunes in a strange land. On the 23rd several officials came on board to inspect the quarters, and, the relatives of captain and crew having departed, the voyage was again resumed. The vicissitudes of the journey from this point are given very geographically by the captain, who ultimately dropped anchor in New York Harbour at 9 p.m. on July 7th. The passage had occupied forty-five days in all, or forty from Newport, whereas the **Mauretania** and **Lusitania** traverse the distance between Fishguard to New York in four-and-a-half days!"

Masters Certificates are mentioned in the article which prompts me to talk about sea captains and education. Every fourth house in Newport was owned or occupied by a mariner. But in Dinas (Dinas Cross) they used to say that every other house was a Captain's house. Dinas was always a cut above Newport, there was much more money there and rich widows in abundance. Even when I visited houses in Dinas in the 1980's the rooms were still lavishly decorated with carved tables, bamboo chairs and ivory ornaments from exotic places like Bombay or Manila. Momentos brought home from afar by a grandfather Captain on his Cape Horner windjammer one hundred years before. Although Tenby seems to have the designation of Pembrokeshire's Jewel in the Crown, those who know Pembrokeshire and Newport know that it is the latter that should hold this touristy title. Newport is unpretentious, it secretly knows it is the best visitor spot in the county. It does not need any honour, badge or banner to advertise itself. The charm and character of the place, its location and stunning beauty maintain its number one spot as a peaceful place for the discerning.

Anywhere else, the Boat Club would be called a Yacht Club. I was at an Inaugural meeting where members agreed that it should not have such a prestigious title. All regarded the membership should be for boating folk, the common man with a love of the sea. To name the Club anything else was not in keeping with Newport culture and its traditions.

I have to add this little ditty, hoping my memory remembers it correctly; it goes like this. ***Newport Nonsense, Dinas Pride, Fishguard Herrings, Goodwick Style.***
Probably coined about 1860, before Fishguard Railway and Harbour was built. This was a time when Goodwick, like a lot of coastal towns in Wales was regarded as a bit of a spa town. It is a typical Pembrokeshire joke, and epitomizes what all in the neighbourhood would think about their neighbours. Dinas Pride relates to all the Captains' houses, Goodwick Style to its upmarket spa beach. Fishguard to its tradition of herring fishing and Newport Nonsense, well, it may relate to the odd characters that abound there.

"Daniel Plant used to collect the rubbish every Saturday, and he was a great character!. He used to say that the weather in this country had never been the same since the Panama Canal was built, and he would stick to that! And, you know the way we change the clocks for summertime and wintertime ? Well this old man used to call it Lloyd George's time (that was summertime) and God's time! He didn't like Lloyd George much and he didn't like the idea of the clocks being moved either." He used to tell the kids stories. "He told them that he once made a harness for his horse and cart out of seaweed. He was carting a load up the hill from Cwm yr Eglwys and the horse arrived home a quarter of a mile ahead of the cart! He looked so serious about it, you know, that kids used to believe him!". Essex Havard related the day when an uncle of his got hold of some gunpowder that his grandfather used to sell for the quarry. There were two old ladies sitting round the fire having a nice gossip and putting their feet up. He quietly sneaked into the house and threw some powder onto the fire. There was a terrible BANG and two horrified screeches! Legs in the air and skirts flying!. "At about the same time, Uncle Essex, my namesake, tried to blow up Newport School.! He was about ten or eleven. It was an abortive thing, but the intention was there! He put the gunpowder under a stone, and it was lucky he didn't lose his eyesight."

*Newport Sand Bar.*

**The Chain Crossing.**
Mention has been made to the depth of the river across the Parrog. Traditionally children were not allowed to go swimming on the Parrog side of the river as it was considered too dangerous. They were always told to swim on Traethmawr or Big Beach were there were no strong river currents. To cross over to the beach, even at low water, had to be done at the "chain".which was always the shallowest crossing route.

Propellers from some of the visiting cargo steamships would help to keep a channel in the river, but this chain had many functions. First of all it defined where the crossing point was. Secondly it was something to tie a sailing vessels to. A permanent mooring that with a cable they could slip when they wanted to leave. With a strong ebb and the river flow it was extremely difficult to anchor any vessel in the river. If vessels anchor on the incoming tide the anchor is unlikely to be effective on the ebb tide which would be twice as strong and going in the opposite direction. Furthermore when the tide floods the vessel floats before there is tension on the anchor cable. The vessel lifts and is moving at at maximum speed in the opposite direction as to when the anchor was set, holding any weight of vessel just does not happen. Additionally the chain would both scour and help deposit gravel on each side of it. It naturally would always lie on the river bed whatever the sand level was on either side of it.

**Culm.**
Looking through the Shipping News during the Victorian era the most common cargo for coastal trading sloops was 'culm'.

One hears a lot about 'Culm' as a cargo and as a fuel for the limekilns. An explanation is needed. The derivation of the word may come from a combination of Old English and Welsh.

Middle English *colme coal dust perhaps from* Old English *col coal.* However Welsh cwlm ("knot or tie"), applied to this type of coal, which is much found in balls or knots in some parts of Wales.

Thus in Wales it has two distinct meanings. If the word is used as a cargo, it refers to the screenings or washings of a coal mine. It is the waste coal dust that may have impurities such as carboniferous limestone or slate. Such impurities are not wanted in coal fuel used in boilers for the trains and ships, ie export coal. The word can also mean small anthracite particles.

As it was so impure it was an ideal fuel to use in the limekilns to make quicklime to neutralize the farming soils. The limekilns were filled with alternate layers of limestone and coal dust (culm) and fired for a week to make quicklime.
The coal dust was also mixed with clay and made into balls to make a convenient fuel for the home fire. This was also called Culm from Welsh cwlm ("knot or tie"), ie binding it together .

The older women gave their memories to the schoolchildren; "The culm or coal dust, that the boats brought in, would be mixed with the clay, to make a cheap and useful fuel. People were bringing clay down from the mountain then, and drying it in the sun. Every house on Parrog had it in front, ready for winter. And then they used to hammer it until it was like powder, and then keep it in boxes. They used about one bucket of clay to seven boxes of culm. Mix it like mortar, then. It was the girl's job on Saturday, very often." Not all the clay used was collected locally. " The **Desdemona** used to come in with a cargo of white china clay, (presumably from Fowey) and I used to cart it away and discharge her. That was the stuff for the fire, and we used to make marbles out of it, and put them in the oven! And we'd have plenty of marbles all the time the china clay lasted!" In Ireland the culm balls were called coal bumbs *(www.sip.ie/sip019B/bumbs/bumbs.htm)* If they were made into a large snowball size there was no need for a grate on the home fire, they would burn slowly in a hearth.

The limekilns would produce a limestone mortar for use in constructing the stone built houses. Quicklime mixed with water would also produce a whitewash used for smartening up the outside of the houses. In the Victorian times most of the Newport cottages and their garden walls were snowy white with a limestone wash. Quicklime was used by the farmers to spread over the fields to improve the soil and to stabilize clay soils.
There are only three Limekilns still remaining close to Newport. One is on the Coast path at Bryncyn, another is in one of the bays to the west and one at the Parrog. There used to be more on the Parrog but these, like at least three warehouses have been removed. One warehouse was removed in 1921 and the stone taken to build the Memorial Hall.
The slate used in the construction of the seawalls around Parrog, came from the sea cliffs to the west of Cat Rock. Most of the slate sea walls were constructed about 1810 to 1840. By the end of the century the sea walls surrounding the present Boat House were in need of major repair. Just next to boat house is a small quay, suitable as a dry dock to build or repair two ships. Adjoining this was a coal store where the culm and coal was stored. On the corner of that spit of land you will see today a large mass of brambles . This used to be the saw pit. Timber was laid across the pit and sawn with a long two man saw. One man would be standing in the pit below and one man on top. Planks for shipbuilding or house flooring were sawn in this way before steam engine saws took over. The curved frames for the ships would be shaped using axes and adzes but all the outer hull of carvel planks would be sawn. Most of the specialized timber for masts and planks for the carvel hulls were collected from the Baltic for the Newport built vessels. We know that one of the Havard ships was sailing to Danzig in 1836 because the master John Havard, only 31 years of age died there. It seems to be a decade later that timber came into West Wales from Canada. Some large timber laden ships entered Cardigan port after 1847 came from Quebec, but this was when shipbuilding at Newport was already on the decline.

**Why a Pole off the Boat club?** Not being able to work out its function I asked Essex what he thought it was put there for. He told me it was to do with the training of the Breeches Buoy with the Cliff Rescue Unit. We may have been talking at cross purposes as there were two poles in 1974. One in the water off the Boat Club and the other on the land at Parrog as seen in the photograph above. I think they may have both been used for Rocket Line practice. The one in the river channel had too many boulders at its base to be useful as a leaning post. It would, however be very useful to tie up to, to temporarily moor a vessel at any state of the tide and to be able to cast off easily from it. Using an anchor in a river estuary is always a problem. Mainly because you need to set two and then you cannot lift one when you wish to depart. There is the added problem of the vessel sitting on it own anchor, springing a bottom plank and sinking. If a permanent mooring or a pole is used, these hazards can be avoided. The Boat Club pole is also a useful aft mooring post, for large vessels moored alongside and for those positioned in the slip.

As the Board of Trade Rocket Line Crew did a practice four times a year, both poles would have been very useful and it was a great public spectacle to see volunteers hauled across the river on a Breeches Buoy. Mortar and rocket apparatus was adopted by the Coastguard in Pembrokeshire in about 1840. The first stone building next to the limekiln was built to house the BOT Rocket Apparatus and its Cart. The next building was the town mortuary.

**Stephen the ferry man,** (picture below) using his short arm with a hook to scull his coffin shaped boat across the river. The water is smooth and the tide must be flooding. When the tide ebbed the river and tide strengths combined made the outflowing current too strong for him to operate.

There were four ferry crossings when enough visitors were around. One penny charge at High Water ½ half a penny at Low Water. Someone noted that the ferry man in this picture is wearing a top hat. This may be a bit more Newport Nonsense or eccentricity but I am sure it encouraged his passengers to give him an extra one penny tip. In the background is a trading ketch that Dillwyn Miles has reported as being the **Newland** a 29 ton, Dandy. The only thing I have found about the **Newland** is that she was a ketch built Tarleton, Lancashire in 1859; registered Belfast; owned by Capt. James Montgomery of Bangor in 1877 and owned by him until his death in 1896. The vessel took limestone and bricks to Ballyhalbert, County Down, Northern Ireland about 1890. I am sure this is the same vessel as the dandy shown against Havard's quay in the photograph below. This indicates that the photo may be taken before 1900 and could be the **Newland** is delivering limestone or bricks to Newport around 1896.

Stephen the ferryman in his coffin shaped boat with the ketch **Newland** unloading limestone next to the Boat Club building.

## Whales

When I was out training with the Cary brothers, (Coedwnog) for our Down River Rowing race we would go out for a rowing practice into Newport Bay and across to Carreg Edrywy. It was a flat calm summer's evening and as we turned to return to Cwm. I was Cox and looking forward and was amazed to see two whales escorting us across the bay. As the rowing boys were just getting into a rhythm I had the dilemma of maintaining the practice session or tell the others about the whales. Our training was of vital importance. The rowers then saw me looking into the water and asked me what I had seen. I told them it was two whales. They continued rowing thinking I had seen two bottlenose dolphins, a relatively common sight in the bay. Only afterwards did I tell them that the whales were twice the size of dolphin and I was still trying to identify which species they were. In the 1970's I remember seeing two whales in the shallow water just outside Lower Fishguard off Saddle Point. They were together and both in excess of 15 feet long. Both Newport and Fishguard would have salmon, a delicacy for the toothed whale species. At the time I was not experienced at observing and identifying whales and did not instantly recognise the fin or back.

Now, having seen whales all over the world from Greenland to Australia, I would have a better chance of identifying them accurately. This is not the first time Whales have been seen in Newport Bay. One of the older woman residents related a story of some local fishermen catching and killing two "porpoises". "One of them was 17 feet long and the other about 12 feet long. They slapped up a tent over them and charged a penny entrance fee! The big one had its nose and tail sticking out! They could not hide all that. They had to kill them or they would have ripped the salmon nets to pieces." Size alone, shows that these were not dolphin.

People say that since the 1880's the Teifi estuary has silted up and that has restricted the passage of large vessels up to Cardigan. The same is said of Newport estuary, but I maintain that the sand bars depth and the river depth have changed little over the centuries. I know that the course of the rivers may change every week. I am also aware of the historical debate about dredging the Teifi but I think the idea was more to do with licences to obtain sand, than to do with navigation.

Captain Crystal George Beer of Sandy Haven fame used to keep two vessels wintering at Newport around the 1910 to 1920 era. In 1910 his name was mentioned at a meeting of the Court Leet. He was one of the culprits taking sand from the Parrog and some Newport merchants were a bit miffed at him doing so on two counts. Firstly they considered the sand removal from the Parrog side of the river could undermine the foundations of the quay walls. Some members had no objection to him removing sand from the Bennet (Beach) side of the river. Other members did not favour any sand removal, unless permission and a royalty was paid to the Lord of the Manor. Beer at first probably told Newport folk it was ballast for his vessels when departing the port. However I am sure it developed into sand as a cargo to Milford that could be sold at a high price as it was already pre-washed so that it could be used for building construction. As Beer would only wanted sand washed with fresh water, the sand on the Parrog side would be preferable as the salt levels would be lower. I am not sure what became of the Court Leet discussion but I would guess that Beer stopped collecting Parrog sand and sought his sand in another estuary.

Captain Beer otherwise affectionately known as Capt Crystal, was in the habit of salvaging any vessel that he could acquire at a bargain price. He was the one who helped Ronald Lockley remove the coal cargo from the **Alice Williams** in 1929, when that schooner was wrecked on Skokholm Island. As Ronald Lockley had farmed Dinas Island before moving to Skokholm, he was probably already familiar with Captain Beer and the ships he brought into Newport.

When the two Morris brothers were interviewed by the school kids in the 1970's, they could relate stories about Newport going back to the 1900-1915 era. They could remember the names of some of the vessels. The **Water Lily, the Kate, Thomas and Anne, the Newland, Garlandstone, the Sambo, the Crystal, the Sarah, New Providence** and the last to be seen in Newport, the **Wave**. (See photo)
Every tide saw the boats coming in, bringing coal, culm and manure for the farmers. They used to unload into carts night and day between the tides. There were always two vessels, each winter on the marsh next to the Parrog Car park. These were ships being repaired for Captain Beer, he had quite a few boats." The ketch **Garlandstone**, mentioned is still to be seen as a Historic Ship floating at Tavistock in Devon .

In Wales the Christian name of the father was carried on by the son as a surname. Thus one of the Newport traders was called Owen Owens. Looking at the names, both family name and given names mentioned above we see George, William, Owen and Griffiths, names still looming large in the Newport area.

The largest wharehouse on the Parrog around 1900, now the Boat Club. Note the large limekiln in the centre of the picture which was still there in 1950.

The ships were built at two locations. Shiphill at the limekiln not far from the iron bridge and on the wet land near the Parrog Car Park. The land is a few feet above normal high water. When built the ships could easily be launched on the Equinoctial tides. The biggest tides each year being the March and September Equinox. On the Newport side of the river, for a few years in the 1980's I used to winter berth my 27 ft fin keel yacht into the mud near the Iron Bridge. It had a draught of over 5 feet and most Spring Tides it would easily navigate the river as far as the Iron Bridge. Once stuck into the soft mud, the yacht was as secure as a bug in a rug. When positioned opposite Bryncyn in October, the depth of water during the winter meant it would have been impossible to sail her out until the Spring.

The Lane pathway from the Iron Bridge to Parrog, is called the "Burma Road". It acquired its name from Essex Havard and others who successfully returned from WWII and found the path hot, sticky, stinking and full of flies. When the town's old refuse tip and the slaughterhouse were relocated the flies and smell departed but the path's nickname remains.

*Photograph of Parrog about 1905.* People are outside The Queen's Hotel in their Sunday best. The rowing boat is similar to "Danny Boy" still being used today.

Will Morris had some memories for the schoolchildren. He was talking of the large families and several members of the same family earning their living on the sea. " Old Captain Hughes of Newport had about ten or eleven boys at sea. They sailed on New Years eve, and they never heard any more about them. Afterwards they didn't like to see too many boys going from the same place." If these boys were all on the same ship it must be a large sailing ship, with a possible crew of 20-30, such as a Barque of Full Rigged Ship sailing foreign from Liverpool, Aberystwyth or Swansea with Captain Hughes as master or mate. Looking through the Hughes family history of Borth we see that there was a David Hughes that was lost at sea in 1865 on the Aberystwyth barque **Glenara** Official Number 36466 the date 22nd July 1865. The same family lost a mariner in the same year that was sailing on the ship **"Spirit of the South"**. When looking for such a ship, I failed to find it and wondered if the Ancestry record saying "Spirit of the South" actually meant **"Spirit of the Seas"** a Liverpool barque that regularly sailed to Singapore. If anyone knows the date when ten Newport youths were lost at sea, please let me know.

**Ship Registration and tonnage measurement.**
British ship registration really began with an Act in 1786. This Act applied to 'all ships having a Deck, or being of the Burthen of fifteen tons, or upwards,' this applying to all British subjects. A major change in ownership, or alterations affecting the tonnage, dimensions or description, involved a registration de novo. The system of tonnage measurement in force at that time was ' Builders' Measurement,' or 'Old Measurement ' as it was later called. This became law by an Act of 1773 (13 Geo. Ill, c. 74), and was then inextricably linked with ship registration. The figure of ' tons burthen ' entered in the ship's register was that on which dues were paid. Newport built ships were registered in Cardigan port which meant that they could enter Newport or Cardigan Port, free of port dues.
From legislation in 1826 all vessel had to put the name of the ship and its registered Port on the transom.

An Act of 1819 (59 Geo. Ill, c. 5) re-enacted this tonnage rule, but incorporated a modification allowing for the deduction, in the case of steam vessels, of engine and boiler spaces for the purpose of tonnage calculation. No doubt this was a considerable encouragement for the rising method of propulsion. A further Act 'An Act for the Registry of Vessels ' (4 Geo. IV, c. 41), and came into force on I January 1824. The property in every vessel of which there are more than one owner, shall be considered to be divided into 64 shares.'1 Unfortunately the practice of charging dues on the registered tonnage of a vessel encouraged builders and owners to take advantage of an obvious loophole in the Builders' Measurement formula, which took no account of the depth of the hold. Porter described it as ' ... the barbarous system which ... Was followed for the admeasurement of shipping, and which enabled the builders, at the sacrifice of some essential good qualities, to procure the official measurement to be greatly below the actual cubical capacity of the hold of the vessel, which capacity it was pretended to insert in the register.' This was said to produce voluminous hulls that sailed badly, and are very unmanageable in bad weather and on a lee-shore. In 1821 and again twelve years later a Committee appointed by the Admiralty investigated the matter of tonnage measurement. As a result .New Measurement ' was instituted and came into force on
 January 1836. This "New Measurement" involved the taking of three depth measurements and two beam measurements. All new ships now had a tonnage measurement to show their cargo capacity.  When recording dimensions and details of a vessel please do not call the Registered Tonnage a *weight*. It is a cargo or hull capacity figure called tons which reflects how much cargo can be carried. It is totally different from the 'weight' of the vessel ie what it would weigh in air if it was lifted on a crane lift.

On some of the vessels listed I have put their dimensions. These were traditionally measured in feet and tenths of a foot. The beam is the measurement from side to side (bulwarks) probably measured at deck level. The depth is not the depth of the hold (keel to deck) but relates to the draught of the vessel when fully loaded with cargo. This depth figure determines if the vessel can get over Newport sandbar at High Water. 13 feet seemed to be the maximum depth. Newport built vessels were usually registered at the port of Cardigan. Cardigan sandbar being a comparative depth to that at Newport. Once registered at Cardigan the vessel could enter Newport or Cardigan port without having to pay Manorial or the usual port dues.

From the different methods of arriving at tonnage we see that the same vessel during its life may start off with a tons burthen old measurement figure and later after say 1850 be assigned a different tonnage. The rig (types of sail and number of masts) may also change throughout the lifetime of the vessel. A brig, a two masted vessel, may change its rig to a Schooner or ketch, then needing less crew to operate her. After 1900 many of the trading vessels would have an auxiliary engine fitted. The tonnage figure was reduced as an engine has now taken up some of the cargo space.

**Types of vessels built at Newport**
These included, Brigs, Brigantines, Snows, Sloops and Schooners. No ships were built bigger than 250 ton s. No barques or full rigged ships were constructed. The size of ships was determined by the depths of their hulls. They needed to be as big as they could for carrying cargos yet shallow enough draft to get over the sand bars at Newport or Cardigan, their home ports. A smack has the same rig as a sloop with a single mast, it was the name given a smaller sloop. A snow was rigged as a brig, but had an additional rudimentary mast stepped immediately aft of the mainmast to carry the fore-and aft mainsail. At a distance this additional mast being immediately next to another is difficult to observe.

This additional mast could not be seen at a distance, although the fore and aft sail it carried could identify the vessel as a Snow. If the vessel was seen at a distance it would look like a brig, especially if the main fore and aft sail was not hoisted. The smallest sailboats were the yawls and dandys. These were commonly seen fishing around the coast of West Wales up to the 1930's. They had a distinctive small mast and sail at the extreme stern of the vessel. In addition to a bowsprit, they would also have a boom sticking out from the stern, called a bumpkin. This would take a loose footed mizzen sail. If you come across a sailor who boasts that he knows all the sailing terms, ask him what a bumpkin is. If he can tell you with confidence, he probably does know a fair bit about sailing rigs. The photograph of the ferry man and the ketch in the background being called a Dandy intrigued me. The position of the masts, to get maximum access to the cargo hold, makes this ketch unusual. As the vessel was more barge like, the term Dandy may have been applied.

Anyone interested in any ancient monument, building or shipwreck in Wales should first have a look what has been included in Coflein Mapping. They describe Newport as a medieval port and …"Originally there was a small fishing community here, and some of the cottages are probably more than 400 years old". That may be so, but it is a mundane description when we now know that it was a major shipbuilding town in 1820's with exports of slate stone from the sea quarries and even importing timber from the Baltic with which to build its ships. Wool, pottery, herring and salmon was also an export in some years. I have often wondered what cargoes were taken out to St Petersburg in Russia. It is only a calculated guess but some years when the herrings were plentiful, it must have been salted herring.

## Cargoes.

In the 1830 to 1860's Newport sloops would be bringing in a variety of general produce. The importations of the port in 1830 was timber, limestone, coal and culm; and its exports were corn, butter, and slates; in some seasons the salmon and herring fisheries were very profitable. Outgoing cargo included slates, herring and oats. Potatoes to and from Ireland and milled corn was also carried as cargoes. It was the days before motor vehicles and the railways. All merchandise travelled by sea. The Railways came to Haverfordwest about 1860 and to Fishguard about 1896. When the weather was favourable there could be 30 sailing vessels in Newport Bay, some waiting to enter and others waiting for the tide to take them up the coast to Aberystwyth. On each high tide the sloops would cross Newport sand bar and deliberately ground their hulls on the sand opposite Parrog inside the harbour when the tide went out. The seamen then had a rest while the land team of horses and carts would work night and day unloading the cargo. Sometimes it took two days to unload a 50 ton smack. The unloading team only getting a sleep when the tide was too deep for the horses to get alongside the vessels. In those days the men who had horses trained to take a wagon deep into the water, ie chest deep for the horse, were the ones that got their cart to the ship first.

## Slate cargoes

The slates loaded as a cargo into the Newport sloops were rough slates quarried from the seacliffs west of Pencatman. They would be used as useful building material but could not be slit thin enough to be used as good roofing slates.

Cilgerran had a better quality slate which could be used for door steps, window cills and hearth slabs. Other slate came out of the quarries on the south banks of the River Teifi, punted down river in shallow draft barges and loaded into the sloops at St Dogmaels.

Using small iron made barges the cut slates were punted down stream from Cilgerran and the slate quarries lining the Teifi. Just upstream of Cardigan town is a shallows which can only be crossed when the tide is full. On Spring tides crossing the shallows would need to be done on the high tide and up to one hour of the ebb. One iron built punt until ten years ago used to be in the Teifi Boat Club car park. The last time I looked it was no longer there. I should have informed the Welsh Maritime Museum of its existence as it could easily have been rescued as a Teifi iron slate barge, probably made in Cardigan about 1835. I don't know of any others remaining from this important part of River Teifi history. Some of the early coal barges near Llanelly were made by the boiler men of iron for use on the early canals of Burry Port.

There are many slate wrecks around the Pembrokeshire coast. I find slate a really interesting commodity and a single slate from a wreck site can give us a lot of information about the identity of the ship lost. The thickness of the slate, its colour and porosity and how it is trimmed and split can immediately tell us if the cargo was from Cardigan or from Caernarfon.

An expert eye can quickly recognise the quarries and ports the ship departed from and a good idea of the date the cargo was lost. All the better quality slates (thinnest with cut edges) accurately sized are from the Llanberis and Penrhyn quarries loaded at Portdinorwic or the roofing slates from Ffestiniog and Llanfrothen quarries outward from Porthmadog.

**The Porthmadog schooners in the era 1860 to 1900 would be taking roofing slates to the expanding** towns and cities of the UK and all over the world including Hamburg, Buenos Aires and Boston. If the slates are rough and thicker and of less quality or random slates of differing sizes then they could be from Cardigan and date pre 1840. I surmise if trading sloops had to leave Newport with no cargo they would collect sea quarried stone as a ballast/ cargo. Such stones were always a useful commodity at any port they traded with as thick slate stone is easy to build with having at least two flat sides.

This book gives details of over 80 vessels that have definitely been constructed in Newport. Others that do the same exercise they may find a handful more. Most of these ships, because they are registered in Cardigan, are recorded in Lloyds as being built in Cardigan. Indeed the Lloyds registers after 1870 gave dimensions and were more accurate in recording the actual place of build, rather than the port it was first registered in. The Cardigan Custom Register pages where the vessel is first registered will give the correct year of building, a description, dimensions and the shareholders. If they were newly registered in Lloyds the date of building is usually one year later than that shown in the Cardigan Board of Trade Log Book.

Newport specialized in building ships with a Brig rig and the average tonnage of those built was 117 tons. Three Newport built brigs were in the 140 to 150 ton range. A few schooners were also built above 130 tons. Vessels of over 120 ton are likely to go 'foreign' ie trade to Portugal or even to Russia. Researching through Lloyds List or the newspapers at shipping news; the name Newport may crop up as a trading port. This will inevitably mean Newport. Monmouth shire (Gwent). There is an added complications with news from USA where Newport then refers to Newport, Rhode Island.

Within this book text, Newport, always means Newport, (Tredraeth) Pembrokeshire. The Lloyds Register of Ships is the definitive annual register of ship details. However you can imagine the confusion when the place name Newport is given as the place of build. It could be either in Pembrokeshire or Gwent. As a general rule if the building date is before 1826, then it will mean Trefdraeth. Those mentioned built after 1826 could refer to either port. The owners and captains surnames have to be referred to in order to clarify the problem.

Occasionally the word *unspecified* is found which means it is difficult to tell which Newport is being referred to.

Lloyds Register may also record Newport built vessels as made in Wales. I am sure this was done because those in London typesetting could not believe the spelling of the coastal town in front of them and did not know how to abbreviate it to fit into the build column in the register. Far easier to say built in Wales than work out which minor beach it may have actually been built on. Smaller coastal villages may have the same name or be difficult to spell. In these instances the port of Registration and the owners give us a clue as to where the vessel was built.

As a general rule if Lloyds lists the vessel as built in Newport **and** it is registered in Cardigan, the vessel will be Pembrokeshire built. If the building location is Wales, then one needs to look at the name of the captain or the port it is registered at. Newport in Lloyds registers after about 1860 usually means Newport. Monmouthshire.

Lloyds Registers can be seen online and a typical entry looks like this . The second **Claudia** on this entry records the Schooner built by Levi Havard in 1835 with D.Griffiths as master.

```
501|Claro      Bk  G. Clarke 348 Sndrld 1850 W.Abbay Sndrlnd Sld.Singapr  10 A 1
               YM.50         401                                             50
  2|Claud      Bk  Buckwell 371 Whtby 1828 Buckwell  Shorhm  Lon.Califin 10 Æ1
    ptZ.51 I.B              Irp.40ien xn. &lrp.50                    8.8.56  55
  3|Claudia    Sk  W Francis 29 Wales 1850 W Francis Aberyst Abs Coaster 6 A 1
               I.B.             O&E.                                        50
  4|—          Sr  DGriffiths 103 N'wprt 1835 Havard & Cardign Mil.Coaster 9 Æ1
               I.B.            89 Srprs 47&50 p txn.50               8.8.56  2
  5|—          Bn  T. Morris 117 Abryst 1850 Morris&c Aberyst Liv Medit. 12 A 1
```

When looking at Lloyds Registers, you needs to familiarize yourself with the abbreviations which are given at the beginning of each Register book. In the above extract **Claudia** is the name of the ship with Sk meaning Smack. The next column is the name of the captain that was master in the preceding year to printing. The 29 relates to the tonnage at last survey. Wales is place of building and in this case 1850 is the build year, or when first added to Lloyds Register, which was often the year after the actual build date. The next column gives the shareholders/owners. In this case it shows Havard &, meaning Havard and Company. Cardigan in the next column shows she is registered in the Port of Cardigan. The last columns show that Mil, (Milford) the abbreviated port is the last Survey Port and 6 A1 is her classification. She was given 6 years of the best classification at her last Lloyds assessment.

## Classification of sail vessel by rig.
Newport vessels would usually be either sloops or brigs. There were few schooners or ketches.

*Sloop* - single masted with main sail fore and aft. Had a bowsprit also carrying for and aft fore sails. A *Smack* is same rig but tends to be a smaller vessel. Some sloops were larger than schooners. Smaller trading vessels would carry a master, a mate and a boy.

*Ketch* - A two-masted fore-and-aft-rigged sailing vessel with a mizzenmast stepped aft of a taller mainmast but forward of the rudder. If the mizzen mast is abaft the rudder it is a *Yawl*

*Schooner* - A fore-and-aft rigged sailing vessel having at least two masts, with a foremast that is smaller or the same height as the other mast.

*Brigantine* - A two-masted sailing ship, square-rigged on the foremast and having a fore-and-aft mainsail with square main topsails. *Snow* is similar but the second mast attached to the main mast, at a distance it looks like one mast with brig rig. .

*Brig* - A two-masted sailing ship, square-rigged on both masts.

*Barque* - A sailing ship with from three to five masts, all of them square-rigged except the after mast, which is fore-and-aft rigged.

*Ship* - A sailing vessel having three or more square-rigged masts.

Although Newport mariners sailed on steamers, barques and full rigged sailing ships, none of these types were built at Newport. There was a sudden decline of ships built in Newport after about 1850. The range of most of the Newport vessels was coastal around the entire coast of UK and Ireland. Many carried goods from Ireland to London or cargoes up to Scotland. Some of the largest vessels of the vessels built at Newport did 'go foreign' and made trips to the Baltic and Arctic circle or to Lisbon. None as far as I can ascertain did Atlantic voyages.

All Newport vessels were sailing vessels made entirely of wood. They had single decks, one or two masted and the ends of the hull planks fastened with iron bolts. The hull was carvel built on wooden frames. Although there were woods in the Nevern Valley, good timber by 1740 was hard to come by for the building of Newport ships. We see that some of the Newport built ships sailed to Danzig in the Baltic, and I believe that this was one purpose only. To return with timber with which to the build the ships. The masts would have been built out of fir trees from the Baltic. Some timber was imported into Cardigan from Prince Edward Isle and Nova Scotia, mainly for house and roof construction. Undoubtedly timber from the Maritimes was also used in the ships built on the River Teifi. However I get the impression that the Havards favoured the Baltic timber, and would sail their ships there in order to choose the correct shipbuilding timbers.

Newport shipbuilders always made sturdy well built ships. This is reflected in the fact that the first and subsequent surveys would often be the A1 Lloyds category. Many of the ships had life spans of 40 years and some over 100 years. Ships made of softwoods in Prince Edward Island would, in comparison, only have a useful life of 20 years. The Newport ships were strong, but also cumbersome, heavy and slow. Their design, had little changed from 1750 to 1850 made for a ship that nobody wanted to buy or sail at the commencement of the Industrial Revolution. Determining which ships were built in Newport Monmouthshire and which in Newport Pembrokeshire is difficult enough, but the whole thing is more complicated when we see that John Havard, master shipbuilder of Newport actually supervised the building of a Brig in Newport Monmouthshire in 1819!

### Brig and Brigantine

A common trading vessel up to about 1840. Two masted with square sails on both masts (Brig) or Square sails on foremast, as in this picture (Brigantine). A basic rig for sailing the Trade winds routes. The square sails act like a spinnaker when the wind is behind you. Carried a crew of ten men for ocean voyages.

**Schooner.** Also 2 masted but both masts with fore and aft sails. Second mast is sometimes taller and carries the main sail. Less crew needed to man them, perhaps 5 men. More manoeuvrable when going into harbour and sailing against the wind. **Ketch** is also two masted but the second (mizzen) mast is much shorter with a smaller Sail.

**Sloop and Smack.** Single mast with all sails for and aft. Crew of 3 men, usually coastal trade not foreign.

**Fishing Lugger.** A traditional rig for West Wales fishermen. The mainsail has no boom (loose footed) so as not to hit the fisherman when he is working amidships. One or 2 men only.

The Port of Cardigan Registers tell us the building details, who the builder was and the shareholders. The Lloyd Ship Register entries do not tell us who the builder was but the name of the master in the second column sometimes gives us a hint. If the master name is Havard or the owners are Havard there is a good chance the vessel was built by Levi Havard or John Havard and Sons. If the captains name is Lloyd, Wade, Williams or Harries the ship was probably made at the William Lloyd yard. Thomas Lloyd was shipbuilder from 1770 to 1790. Then William Lloyd took over the business.

The following pages list the **ships built at Newport.** They are in date order of the launch date. This means chronological order rather than alphabetical.

**Ann and Mary** Built Newport 1762. Sloop 17 tons. In the Cardigan Register in 1787/32 Mentioned by Barbara George in the early Port Books. Lost when 111 yrs old at St David's Head on 25 April 1873 . Wind NNE force 6. The same gale caused another Newport vessel, **Fly,** to be lost 15 miles offshore from Fishguard with all 3 crew.

**Speedwell of Llanelly** Built Newport 1765 Sloop 29 ton In the Llanelly Register in 1786 no 23. Entered into the Liverpool Register on 15 May 1788. In Lloyds 1776 there is a 50 ton sloop built in Wales in 1767 with master William Evans as owner/captain, She was last surveyed in Bristol and sailing to Belfast. A **Speedwell** was lost in Cardigan Bay with a master Jones. She was sailing from Newry and lost in April 1810. A **Speedwell** 65 ton vessel built in Wales in 1786, which may or not be the same vessel

**Mary** Built or rebuilt at Newport 1773. Sloop 24 tons. In Cardigan Register 1786 no 9. BT6 /191 AL 91:92 Not seen in Lloyds 1776.

**Rose of Newport** . Built at Newport 1773, Sloop, 22 ton. In Cardigan Register 1787 no. 152. BT6/ 191 Al 91:92.
Dimensions: 38.6 feet long, 12.6 ft beam and 6.3 ft draught.
Not in Lloyds 1776 or 1808.

**Little Speedwell of Newport.** Built at Newport 1776, Sloop, 18 ton. In Cardigan Register 1787 no. 124. BT6 /191. Dimensions 36.8 feet long 11.6 ft beam and 5.9 ft draught.

**Betty of Newport**. Built at Newport in 1777. Sloop. 24 ton. In Cardigan Register in 1807 no 2 and Cardigan Register in 1825 no.53. In Lloyds Register of 1834 Betty 26 ton sloop of Cardigan. D, Jenkins, master This may be another vessel as my records for the Newport built sloop is 'Lost 1829'. A **Betty** was lost near Dublin on a voyage Bridgwater for Belfast in 1818.

**Providence** Built at Newport in 1777, Sloop, 28 ton. In Cardigan Register in 1811 no 20 at 26 ton. Additional information via Glen Johnson **Providence** (St. Dogmaels) Sloop 28 tons. Built, 1777 Newport. In 1826, her master was Captain Thomas Thomas. In January 1807 there was a **Providence** lost near to St David's Head sailing from Youghall to Swansea, that had a captain Thomas, all crew saved.
This would seem to be the correct vessel but next to this entry I originally had a note that she was lost in 1848. The confusion remains.

**Mermaid.** Sloop 28 ton . Taken as a prize in 1777. Thought to have been rebuilt in St Dogmaels in 1778. Newport owners . On 8th December 1807 **Mermaid** a sloop of Newport carrying a cargo of culm with Thomas Lloyd master was lost at Whitesands, St David's *(Cambrian newspaper 19 Dec.1907).* Not to be confused with the 25 ton sloop **Mermaid,** Barmouth built in 1798 master Griffith.

Unloading from the schooner **Wave** about 1920.

**Nightingale.** Built at Newport in 1778. Sloop, 40 ton. In Cardigan Registers of 1787 no.6 and 1796 no. 1796 no. 26. (51 ton sloop) BT6/191 Al 91: 92 . Dimensions: 47.8 feet length, 15.4 ft beam and 7.8 ft depth. Possibly lost Liverpool 16 April 1811. Seen in Lloyds 1791 as master D,Davis and owner as E.Bowen 40 ton sloop built 1778. She is recorded in 1793 Lloyds as 50 ton Sloop built in Wales in 1778. Master is crossed out and is difficult to read but could be D.Omara.(Irish name) and replaced with T.Mathias that year. Owner Captain & Co. Operating Newry to London. Not seen in 1808 Lloyds Register.

**Mary** Built or rebuilt at Newport 1781. Sloop 21 ton. In Cardigan Register 1786 no 33.   BT6 /191  AL 91:92. Dimensions: 40 feet long. In 1793 Lloyds there is a **Mary** built in Wales in 1781 a 50 ton Sloop that had Kelly as master and changed to J.Roberts that year. Operating London to Waterford.


**Speedwell.** Built or rebuilt at Newport 1782. Sloop 24 ton. In Cardigan Register 1786   no 10. BT6 /191  AL 91:92 Dimensions: 40.6 feet long, 12.9 ft beam and 6.4 feet depth.  A **Speedwell** was sunk in Cardigan Bay in April 1810 with a Captain Jones sailing from Newry, Ireland. No loss of life recorded. Not sure if same vessel but quite likely.

**Lord Nelson.**  Built at Newport 1782. Snow. 107 ton.  In Cardigan Register 1802 no. 34, (102 ton). In Milford Register in 1811 no.2 , 1814 no. 2, 1825 no.55. Lloyds Register 1834. Lost 1840. In November 1835 the vessel **Spring** was in collision with another vessel called **Lord Nelson** off Flamborough Head ,Yorkshire. **Spring** sank but all crew saved . "Ship News". The Standard (2644). 30 October 1835. Not known if the same **Lord Nelson** built 1782. Many Cardigan brigs of a similar size were doing coastal voyages on the East Coast at this time. There could be two **Lord Nelso**n both of similar tonnage built at Newport.

**Anna Maria** . Built at Newport before 1787, Sloop. 51 ton. In Cardigan Register 1787 no. 93 . There was also an **Anna Maria** that was Newport owned that was built at Aberdovey in 1784, sloop of 47 ton. Perhaps the same vessel.  It is  not known if it the same vessel but in Lloyds List on 1st December 1795 reported **Anna Maria,** master Morris, from London to Barmouth is totally lost near Milford, the Captain and two men drowned.

**Two Brothers.** Built at Newport before 1787, Sloop. 47 ton. In Cardigan Register 1787 no. 95.  There is sloop of this name registered in Lloyds Register in 1792 with master and owner as H.Phillips built in Wales in 1772 and given as 35 ton. Operating Bristol to Youghal. This is difficult to research but the vessel does not appear to be in Lloyds Register in 1793.

**Providence**  Built at Newport 1783 Sloop. 24 ton . In Cardigan Register 1786 no.21  BT 6/191. Al 91:92.  Lloyds Register of 1793 has a Providence built 1784 in Wales 30 ton Sloop, with Captain /owner as W.Morris. She was A1 classed and is likely to be the same vessel.  Two Providence sailing vessels were lost on the Pembrokeshire coast in January 1814, but I do not know if either were the Newport built one.

**Mary** . Built at Newport 1783.  Brigantine 53 ton In Cardigan Register 1787 no.14.  BT 6/191. Al 91:92.  Dimensions: 57.0 feet long, 16.2 ft beam and 8.1 ft depth. Lloyds Register 1792 has a Mary sloop of this tonnage made in Wales in this year but no Brigantine .Lloyds Register 1812 has **Mary** 56 ton sloop built in Wales in 1785 with D.Philipps as master and owner. Classified E2 trading London to Newry, Ireland. It would seem unusual to me for a Brigantine to be changed to a sloop rig.

**Catherine of Newport.** Built or rebuilt at Newport 1784. Sloop. 21 ton . In Cardigan Register   BT 6/191. Al 91:92  Rebuilt at Newport 1785. Dimensions: 40.3 feet long, 12.3 ft beam and 6.1 ft draught. A **Catherine** with Captain Roberts came ashore at Fishguard in a January 1793 gale. She had come from Drogheda, Ireland.  Lloyds List 18. 01.1793.


**Fair Briton.**  Built at Newport 1784, Sloop, 66 ton. In Cardigan Register 1787 no.5 and 1789 no. 14.   In Lloyds Register 1792 as A1 condition built Wales in 1784, sloop 66 ton master T.Jenkins and owner Williams.  Lost January 1809 (?).

**Fair Briton** .  Built at Newport in 1785,  Seen in Lloyds in 1802 as 45 ton Sloop built in Wales in 1790, captain Stevenson, owner Mc Cunn. Sailed to Lisbon. Probably taking wine to Liverpool.   The master and owners do not seem to fit in with a Newport Pembrokeshire vessel.

**Mary of Milford.** Built at Newport 1785. Sloop. 50 ton.  In Milford Register  1786 no.43,  Cardigan Register 1873 no 10.    In Lloyds 1804, there is a **Mary** 48 ton built in Wales in 1785 owner and captain, E1 classified, trading Wales to Dublin. Liverpool


**Flora of Newport** .  Built Newport 1785. Sloop. 28 ton. 38 feet long. Not seen in Lloyds in 1820 or 1827. Not in Lloyds Register in 1801. Lost off Milford 1829.

**Phoenix.**  Built Newport 1785. Sloop. 24 ton. In Cardigan Register 1786. no.32. BT 6/191. Al 91:92 Dimensions: 42 foot length, 12 ft beam and 6 ft depth.  Not in Lloyds Register in 1801.

**Nancy of Newport**   Built at Newport 1785, Sloop, 19 ton. In Cardigan Register 1787 no 53/12. Dimensions: 37.3 feet long, 12.3 ft beam and 6.1 ft depth.  My notes also had **Nancy**. Built Newport 1786 . Sloop. 29 ton. But I think it is the same vessel.

A **Nancy,** captain Morris, was totally lost near Milford on 22nd April 1819  taking a cargo of coal from Newport, Monmouthshire to Belfast .Capt Morris and crew saved. Although this is likely to be the correct vessel, there were numerous sloops with this name.

Another **Nancy of Cardigan** was lost carrying coal. She sank 2 miles West of Newport, Monmouthshire in 1825 on a voyage to Cork.  Without further research it is not clear if either of these losses is the Newport **Nancy.**

**Benjamin of Milford.**  Built at Newport 1785 . Sloop. 64 ton. In Milford Registry 1787 no.12.   In the Lloyds Register of 1795 there are two **Benjamin** listed as being built in Wales. I assume the Newport built one is listed as Sloop, 40 ton, built Wales 1786. Master L Phillips with owner as Williams. Trading Cork to Penzance.  Missing from Lloyds in 1808 so may have been lost before this date.


**Bee.** Built at Newport 1785. Sloop 70 ton.   There may have been two vessels built about the same time called **Bee.**  In Cardigan Register 1787 no.11. Milford Register 1787 no. 48. In Lloyds 1795 as Bee, 70 ton sloop, built 1785. G Lloyd as master and owner. Classified AL, London to Dublin. In Cardigan Register 1808 no.3. In 1785 seen in Lloyds as 50 ton Sloop built in Wales 1785, T.Williams master and Williams as owner.  She was still afloat in 1808 as she was listed in Lloyds as 70 ton sloop Welsh built sloop **Bee** with master T.Owens that was surveyed in Cork and traded to Plymouth.

**Bee**  In Lloyds Register of 1819 we see a 66 ton sloop built at Newport in 1784 with J.Davis as captain and E.Davies as owner. To complicate matters in the same year there are also a 28 ton and a 51 ton sloops also named **Bee** in Cardigan Register. In 1820 Lloyds a sloop of 60 ton built in Wales in 1785 with E.Jones master and J.Jones as owner.

On 7th December 1821 there was a Sloop **Bee** that was wrecked near Holyhead, master Raymond, Liverpool to Cork with salt. Crew saved. As the Newport built Sloop is still in the Lloyds in 1822 it looks like the Holyhead wreck was a different vessel. Another **Bee** was wrecked near Annalong 23rd December 1848 in Ireland. A sloop of the same name lost on 9th January 1819. The Sloop struck the pier at Sunderland, County Durham and sank.

**Fanny of Newport.** Built at Newport 1786. Sloop. 33 ton. In Cardigan Register 1787 no.19.   BT6 /191  Dimensions: 47 feet long 14.4 ft beam and 7.2 ft depth. Lloyds Register 1804 has a Fanny sloop built in Wales in 1786 of 35 tons with T.Harris as master and Griffith & Co. Owner, the following year W.George as master and E.Griffith as owner. Same master and owner in 1791. Usual voyages Wales to Cork or Liverpool / Greenock. Loss date unknown.

**Martha of Abercastle.** Built at Newport 1786. Sloop. 29 ton. In Cardigan Register 1787 no.173. BT6 /191.

**Jolly of Newport**. Built at Newport 1786. Sloop. 24 ton. In Cardigan Register 1786 no.8  BT 6 /191  No record in 1792. Not in Lloyds 1805.

**Prince of Wales.** Built at Newport 1786. Sloop. 49 ton. In Cardigan Register 1787 no.85. BT6 /191 Dimensions: 52.5 feet long, 16.6 ft beam and 8.3 ft depth. My notes also had **Prince of Wales of Fishguard**. Built at Newport 1776. Sloop. 52 tons but I have failed to verify this entry. **Prince of Wales** Built at Newport 1786 Sloop. 49 tons . This is what my original database said. However 1804 Lloyds has other sizes of Welsh built vessel also built about this time. One is a sloop of 103 ton built in Wales in 1787 with D.Evans as master and Evans and Co as owners. The smallest sloop of this name afloat at that time was a 40 ton vessel built in Wales in 1784, in 1793 her master was Cummings and her owner Williams. She did a voyage to Lisbon.

**Betsey of Bristol.** Built at Newport 1785. Sloop, 50 ton. Lloyds Ship Register 1794 lists a **Betsy** at 50 ton Sloop built in Wales last registered in 1789 and 10 years old. Her owner was Evans and Co. and her captain was D. Evans. This is very likely the **Betsy** built in Newport, and she traded between Cork and London. In 1801 Lloyds Register there is a 51 ton sloop **Betsy** built in Wales that was last surveyed in 1798 in Dublin, Capt Jones owner Morris. Trading Dublin to Drodhega. In 1808 Lloyds there is a 61 ton sloop with a captain and owner as G.Morgan , trading Dublin and Waterford.

Built in Wales in 1784 Brig **Betsy** 146 ton likely built Newport as the vessel is in Lloyds Register in 1795 with D. Davis as master and Williams as owner. Classified A1 operating Liverpool to Leghorn.
It is not known if this is the same **Betsey**, but Bristol was one of the main slave trade ports and this sloop was likely to be part of it.

On 28 April 1796. The sloop **Betsey,** commanded by Captain James Peters arrived at Freetown harbour. Zachary Macaulay, in Knutsford, Life and Letters, pp. 133~34, called Peters, 'one of the worst and most profligate wretches I have ever seen in this country.' Afzelius. Journal, p. 153, reported that Peters was anchored so near to Freetown that some feared that he might raid that city for slaves. The Providence Gazette reported that **Betsey** cleared port on 27 November 1795. bound for Africa. This may not be the same **Betsey.**

**Anna Maria** . Built at Newport before 1787, Sloop. 50 ? ton. In Cardigan Register 1787 no. 93 . There was also an **Anna Maria** that was Newport owned that was built at Aberdovey in 1784, sloop of 47 ton. In 1793 Lloyds has a **Anna Maria** built in Barmouth 1784 of 80 tons owned by Davis &Co with a master R.Morris. Classed A1.

**Two Brothers.** Built at Newport before 1787, Sloop. 47 ton. In Cardigan Register 1787 no. 95. There is sloop of this name registered in Lloyds Register in 1792 with master and owner as H.Phillips built in Wales in 1772 and given as 35 ton. Operating Bristol to Youghall.

In 1867 there was a Smack **Two Brothers of Cardigan**, master Jones that was taking slate from Bangor to Bristol. She met bad weather off the Bishops (St David's) and the vessel started taking in water. In a disabled state the Smack was driven towards the Irish coast and just before the vessel foundered, the crew escaped in their own rowing boat. The crew all landed safely at Kingston, but the vessel sank off Wicklow. Precis from *Leeds Mercury 9th January 1867.*

*www.irishshipwrecks.com/shipwrecks.php?wrecksPage=14*

**Dimensions of Newport vessels built (* rebuilt) 1773 to 1789**

| Built | Name | Tons | Type | Length | Beam | Depth |
|---|---|---|---|---|---|---|
| 1773 * | Mary | 24 tons | Sloop | 40.6 | 12.9 | 6.4 |
| 1782 * | Speedwell | 24 ton | Sloop | 40.6 | 12.9 | 6.4 |
| 1783 | Providence | 24 ton | Sloop | 41.0 | 12.11 | 6.5 |
| 1785 | Phoenix | 24 ton | Sloop | 42.5 | 12.4 | 6.2 |
| 1781 | * Mary | 21 ton | Sloop | 40.6 | 12.0 | 6.0 |
| 1778 | Nightingale | 40 ton | Sloop | 47.8 | 15.4 | 7.8 |
| 1785 | Nancy | 19 ton | Sloop | 37.3 | 12.3 | 6.1 |
| 1783 * | Mary | 53 ton | Brigantine | 57.0 | 16.2 | 8.1 |
| 1786 | Fanny | 33 ton | Sloop | 46.11 | 14.4 | 7.2 |
| 1786 | Nancy | 29 ton | Sloop | 42.6 | 14.0 | 7.0 |
| 1787 | Providence | 25 ton | Sloop | 40.3 | 13.2 | 6.7 |
| 1785 * | Catherine | 21 ton | Sloop | 40.3 | 12.3 | 6.1 |
| 1786 | Prince of Wales | 49 ton | Sloop | 52.5 | 16.6 | 8.3 |
| 1776 * | Little Speedwell | 18 ton | Sloop | 36.8 | 11.6 | 5.9 |
| 1773 | Rose | 22 ton | Sloop | 38.6 | 12.6 | 6.3 |
| 1786 | Martha | 29 ton | Sloop | 33.0 | 13.0 | 6.6 |

A curious entry was seen in the Cambrian Newspaper dated January 1819. "On Friday last was launched from the yard of Messrs Hughes and Powell of Newport (Monmouthshire) a fine new Brig called the **Mary and Elinor,** built for Capt. Evan Davis. The vessel is allowed by the first nautical judges to be handsome and well built, of the very best materials, under the direction of that well known builder, Mr John Havard of Newport, Pembrokeshire. She went off in fine style to the gratification of hundreds of spectators."

It is complicated enough to search for the vessels to see if they were built in Newport Pembrokeshire or Newport, Monmouthshire. (Gwent). The complication is now compounded and made more confusing when we know that the boatbuilding at both places was being conducted by the same John Havard!

**Nancy of Newport.** Built at Newport 1786. Sloop. 29 ton. In Cardigan Register 1787    BT6 /191 . Dimension: 42.6 feet long, 14.0 ft beam and 7.0 draught. Not sure if same vessel but there was a **Nancy** of Cardigan lost with coal cargo sailing from Newport, Monmouthshire for Cork. Lost 2 miles West of Newport. Gwent in 1825. Lloyds Register has a sloop **Nancy** built in Wales in 1786 with a master Sambrook listed in 1792 of 32 ton usually sailing Swansea.

**Prince of Wales**   Built at Newport 1786  Sloop. 49 tons . This is what my original database said . However 1804 Lloyds has other sizes of Welsh built vessel also built about this time.  One is a sloop of 103 ton built in Wales in 1787 with D.Evans as master and Evans and Co as owners.  The smallest sloop of this name afloat at that time was a 40 ton vessel built in Wales in 1784, in 1793 her master was Cummings and her owner Williams. She did a voyage to Lisbon.

**Dolphin**   Built at Newport in 1787. Sloop 59 ton In Cardigan Register 1788 no 1 . Cardigan 1798 no.1 Lloyds Register 1792 gives her master as Pritchard and her owner as W. Bowen. She was classified as A1 and one voyage was Bristol to Belfast.  In Lloyds Register 1804 there is a sloop **Dolphin** built in Wales in 1787 with C Bowen as owner and D.George as master, undoubtedly the same vessel. Trading Wales to Liverpool. In November 1803 there was sailing vessel of this name lost in Beaumaris Bay, Anglesey sailing from Newry to Liverpool.  This could be the same vessel, and still be in Lloyds six months later.

**Betsey of Milford**    Built at Newport  1787 . Sloop. 54 ton .  In Milford Register in 1888 no 4.  In Lloyds Register of 1808 there is a **Betsy** sloop of  40 tons, built in Wales in 1787, captain and owner R.Moon, trading Dublin to Bristol.  It was reported on 4th January 1820 that a **Betsey** of Pembroke is lost near Solva. She was taking salt and shop goods from Liverpool to Pembroke. Crew Saved.

Another **Betsy** is seen in the 1808 Lloyds, built in Wales in 1784 of 150 tons a Brig. Repaired in 1800. Shury captain, Gardner owners, operated from London and was used as a Transport. The newspaper Mercury (number 1553) dated 3$^{rd}$ January 1820, gives details of a **Betsey** of Pembroke that was lost with passengers was wrecked on the Traeth Bar, Carmarthen on 8th January 1819 with the loss of seven lives. Two survivors were reported. She was on a voyage from Waterford to Bristol, Gloucestershire. Captain Bevan was amongst those that drowned.

There is much detective work needed to determine which Betsy is which as in the 1794 Lloyds there were 94 ships with such a name listed, no less than 9 of which were built in Wales. All 94 were under Betsy and not Betsey. In 1795 Lloyds Register there are 3 Betsys built in Wales. Although Betsy (Betsey) is a common name within many of the UK Registers it is quite likely that the Newport built ones would be lost within 25 years of build and in the local trading area. To help others looking up Betsey Lloyds List newspaper 16$^{th}$ January 1795 mentions **Betsey** foundered, Master Reeve. The ship was run down and sunk. Her crew were rescued by **HMS Adventure** (Man O'War Royal Navy) and taken to Ireland. **Betsey** was on a voyage from Livorno, Grand Duchy of Tuscany to London. Looking through the extensive list of **Betsys**, we find this one was built in Whitby and was a Brig of 112 tons, so not the one built in Wales.

**Fanny and Mary**. Built at Newport 1787. Sloop. ? ton. In Cardigan Register 1787 . BT6 /191   Not seen in 1802 Lloyds.

**Providence.** Built at Newport 1787. Sloop. 25 ton. In Cardigan Register 1787 no.44.   BT6 /191. AL 91  Dimensions: 40.3 feet long, 13.2 ft beam and 6.7 feet depth. In 1793 Lloyds has recorded a Sloop **Providence**, built in Wales in 1785 that had an owner and captain as Rd (Rodney?) James.  A sailing vessel of this name went aground in Dublin Harbour in 1803 on a voyage from Liverpool to Wexford.   On 21st February 1819 there was a sailing vessel of this name, master Robertson,  that was driven on shore and wrecked at Hubberston Pill with bagged flour and oats from Cork to Bristol.  Also there was a report from near St Ives of a **Providence**, Owen ,David of Swansea, ashore, crew drowned 2nd November 1823.  Further research is needed to determine if any of these were the sloop built in 1787.

**Lovely Peggy.** Built at Newport 1787. Sloop. 29 ton. In Cardigan Register 1787 no.160   Cardigan 1799 no 8  23 ton BT6 /191. Al 91. Lloyds Ship Register in 1804 and 1805 has a **Lovely Peggy,** built 1798  of 50 ton owned by D.George and master W.George.  It is quite likely that this is a different **Lovely Peggy,** as there were three Cardigan ships operating with this name.

**Peggy of Carmarthen**. Built in Newport in 1787. Sloop. 21 ton. In Llanelly Register 1792 no. 8. 1802 no. 14. 1825 no.54. Some confusion here as Lloyds Register of 1801 has a 103 ton sloop built Wales in 1787 with master as D.Evans and owners Evans. And also a 35 ton sloop, built 1790 Wales, R.Jones master and R.Roberts owner . In November 1801 the 32 ton **Peggy** of Newport, Pembrokeshire, ran aground on the Cardigan Bar en route to Bristol from Liverpool with a cargo of salt.  Not to be confused with the **Peggy** that was lost on 2nd October 1841 the 27 ton sloop (built in 1782)  lost on Cardigan Bar en route from Caernarfon to Milford Haven.

**Keturah**. Built at Newport 1787. Brigantine. 113 ton. In Cardigan Register 1787 no.167   BT6 /191. Dimensions: 49.0 feet long, 19.6 ft beam. This had Newport owners. What is somewhat confusing is that there was a **Keturah** built or rebuilt in Cardigan at this time, that was a Brig with Dimensions: 58 feet long 20 feet beam but a smaller tonnage of 88 tons. This had Cardigan owners, sometimes spelt Ceturah this was the first brig built by Levi Havard. See memorial 782. In January 1793 there was a **Keturah**, Captain Gilbert, that got on shore in Fishguard Roads. Although Capt Gilbert lost his life I do not think the ship was wrecked on this date as there is a vessel of this name in 1805. Lloyds Register in 1792 lists **Keturah** built in Wales in 1787 master and owner D. Gilbert. Brig 105 ton. Voyage from Bristol. The Cardigan **Keturah** was still in Lloyds in 1804 and 1805, Keturah, 88 ton brig, built 1787, J.Davies master and Willing & Co owners. One **Keturah**, was lost on 6th April 1885 with notes on financial payments, but a different vessel.
(*Merioneth Archives*)

**Speedwell.** Built at Newport in 1788. Sloop 13 ton . In Cardigan Register 1788 no. 18. BT/6 191. Lloyds Register in 1792  lists other **Speedwell** Sloops built in Wales; one of 50 tons built 1784 with master and owner as W. Davis. And another a 45 ton sloop master built 1788 master D.Jones probably from Aberdovey.

**John.**   Built at Newport 1789. Sloop. 35 ton. Cardigan owned . In Cardigan Register 1789 no.16, Cardigan 1794 no 17  BT6 /191. AL 91:92.   Not to be confused with a 30 ton sloop built at Cwm yr Eglwys in 1820. In October 1797 there was a **John** lost on Caernarfon Bar, Captain Mollyneaux, Liverpool to Dublin. In 1831, 19th January, there was a **John,** Captain James taking wheat and oats from Cardigan to Bristol that got upon an anchor and sunk. Ie. While drying out in Milford Haven she sat on another's anchor which damaged her hull.  Cargo was discharged.

**Jane of Goodwick** Built at Newport 1790, 70 ton Sloop, In Cardigan Register 1790 no.12. Her master was lost at sea in November 1798 and the vessel may have been lost at the same time. She is not in Lloyds Register in 1802 which may suggest she was lost in November 1798. However there was a **Jane** lost in August 1833 that we know was a Newport vessel. .Note; there was another **Jane** built at Newport in 1837, although similar tonnage was Schooner rigged.

**William & Anne of Cardigan.** Built at Newport 1790. Sloop, 90 ton./ 88 ton. In Cardigan Register 1790 no.14. AL 91:92. Cardigan 1812 no.6. 25/125. She is seen in Lloyds Register 1810 as a 91 ton Sloop. R.Morris Captain/owner. built in Wales 1790. A Thomas Morris, possibly son of R.Morris, was buried in St Mary's Churchyard " Died 1819.01.09. Aged 32. (Memorial stone 38) As the vessel is not seen in the Lloyds Register the following year. It is quite possible that the vessel was lost with her crew in that year, somewhere along the Welsh or Irish coast. However, I have searched my records and although this is a common name for a vessel I have failed to find anything else on the vessel's fate or where she was lost.

**Twins**. Built at Dinas in 1790. Newport owners, Sloop, 22 ton. Dimensions: 37.0 feet long 12.7 feet beam, 6.1 feet draught. No other information. Not seen in Lloyds Register but she is a small vessel and may not have been insured. (*Source Robin Craig number 10*)

**Menai.** Built at Newport in 1792. Sloop 70 tons. Her master in 1819 was J. Bowen and owners Lloyds & Co. He was still master when he was lost with all his crew off Rhossilli on 22$^{nd}$ January 1825. The ship was lost and timber (presumably wrecked hull timbers) and her cargo of oats floated ashore near Llanelli. *(Cambrian 22 Jan 1825)*

Built in 1811 this is the Brig/schooner **Maria** of Aberystwyth. At 84 tons she is smaller than the Brigs built in Newport. Note that the foremast carries a foresail, fore topsail (split into two sails) fore top gallant sail also split into two sails, and a small fore royal. It is a somewhat unusual rig and would require a large crew to handle her.   Photo © Nick Tudor-Jones

**Hope**  Brig  129 tons.  Not known where originally built but this ship was Condemned as a Prize in 1799 and was then in the Cardigan registry in 1825. Possibly repaired in Newport and likely Newport ownership. On 6th October 1856 while on a voyage from Llanelli to Limerick a 16 year old lad John Volk lost his life and was then buried in the churchyard at Newport. (Memorial 398).  I have not found out where, but the ship was wrecked at the same time.

**Elizabeth & Mary of Newport.** Built at Newport 1792. Sloop, 56 ton. In Cardigan Register 1792 no.3 . In Lloyds Ship Register of 1801 she is registered with D.Thomas as master/ owner. In 1827 ( the year before she was lost) the Lloyds Register shows D.Jones as master and D.Owens as owner. A severe gale on 11th February 1828 took two vessels ashore near the entrance to Milford Haven. The vessels were completely wrecked and their cargoes could not be saved. One was the **Elizabeth and Mary**, master David James, of Newport. A Milford news stated on 12th February ..."she also got on shore here at the entrance to the Port, and it it is expected that both ship and cargo will be totally lost. Crew saved" Five days later a report said " which was driven on shore at Sheep Island had been dragged into deep water and will be lost with the cargo" The sloop was from Cardiff to Guernsey with a cargo of coal and glass bottles. Searching today amongst the rocks on the Milford Haven side of the rocks below Sheep Island you will find pieces of glass bottles amongst the boulders. If these are from this lost cargo it is difficult to tell. Master David James of Newport lost his life when his ship got wrecked leaving Ann (born 1804) a widow. The other crew members were saved. She was owned by both Newport and Cardigan merchants.
*Strangers from a Secret Land by Peter Thomas . Gomer Press.*

**Elizabeth of Newport.** Built at Newport 1793. Sloop, 54 ton. In Cardigan Register 1793 no.5  AL92

**Rose.**  Built at Newport 1793. Sloop, 25 ton. In Cardigan Register 1803,no.19. Dimensions: 38.6 feet long, 12.6 ft beam and 6.3 ft depth.  In 1799 there was a **Rose** of Cardigan wrecked in Youghal Bay in Ireland. Glen Johnson has a **Rose** Sloop 32 ton built 1798 Cardigan. Perhaps this was lost in Ireland one year after building. The Newport vessel was in a Cardigan Register book four years later. In 1801 Lloyds there is a **Rose In June** built in Wales 1792 but 51 ton, master D.Evans and owners Capt & Co.  Operating to Liverpool.  Not seen in Lloyds 1808.
*www.irishwrecksonline.net/Lists/CorkListG.htm*

**Venus of Cardigan**. Built at Newport 1794. Sloop, 35 ton. In Cardigan Register 1794 no.18. Not seen in Lloyds 1808.

**Flora** Built at Newport 1795. Sloop, 27 ton. 38 feet long.In Cardigan Register 1795 no. 23. Not in Lloyds in 1802, 1808 or 1812. Built by John Havard and his son Levi. Lost off Milford 1829.

**Catherine** Built at Newport 1795. Smack .21 ton . Registered in Cardigan . Larn Shipwreck Database gives details of a Cardigan **Catherine,** built in Cardigan in 1797 of 23 ton that sank off Mumbles on 1st December 1896. Ie 99 years old, Her owner captain was O.Williams from Mumbles. Same vessel? A smack of this name was wrecked in Dundrum Bay 16 Nov 1825; 4 crew rescued by Rossglass Lifeboat Also Fishguard Lifeboat saved crew from **Catherine of Cardigan** in 1880 off Goodwick. It is not known if either vessel is the Newport built one.

**Eleanor**. Built at Newport 1795. Sloop, 51 ton. In Cardigan Register 1796 no.2. Cardigan 1822 no.1. In 31 October 1823 there was a vessel of this name that was wrecked at Fishguard. Lloyds List records. **Eleanor** of and from Fishguard with a local master Davis, was wrecked while trying to enter Fishguard harbour in storm conditions. All crew saved. On the same night the vessel **Nancy** of Liverpool, master Evans, was also lost in Fishguard Bay doing the same thing, unfortunately all were lost.

**Neptune of Milford.** Built at Newport 1797. Brigantine. 60 ton. In Milford Register 1798 no.1. Not seen in Lloyds Register in 1801,so may have been lost within three years of being built. Another **Neptune** was lost en route from Newport to Chester in May 1870. She was a 19 ton sloop built at Lawrenny in 1828 (Reg No. 25264) and as trading from Newport probably had Newport owners.

**Charlotte of Newport.** Built at Newport 1798. Sloop. 36 ton. In Cardigan Register 1798 no.7. In Lloyds 1802, there is a 40 ton Sloop built in Wales in 1774, with Captain/owner as Sullivan. Not seen in Lloyds in 1808. I have not researched further but there was a **Charlotte** a sloop; wrecked at Tyrella, Ireland, all hands lost 14th November 1835. Note there was at least one other vessel with this name built in Newport, but schooner rigged (2 masted) not a single masted.

**Nancy of Newport.** Built at Newport 1798. Sloop. 64 ton. In Cardigan Register 1799 no.1. Cardigan 1805 no.16. There was a **Nancy** sloop lost at Newport Pembrokeshire on 23rd October 1840. *(Deadly Perils book by Peter B.S. Davies ISBN: 9780951520727)* Quite likely same vessel no other details.

**Ardent.** Built at Newport 1800. Snow. 120 ton. In Cardigan Register. In 1812 Lloyds there is a Brig 120 tons built Wales 1800 with Peters as master and Spear and Co as owners. It is unclear if it is the same vessel but there was an **Ardent** lost on the Patches rocks between Cardigan and Aberystwyth in February 1833. With a master Jones carrying coal from Cardiff to Liverpool she was driven onto the Patches during a heavy gale from the NNW. "It is feared will be wrecked, the stern is already knocked in." Lloyds List 26. 02. 1833. Another **Ardent** schooner 125 ton was built at Newport in 1817.

**Samson (Sampson)** Built at Newport 1800. Brigantine. 121 ton. In Milford Register 1800 no.12 and Milford 1802 no.20. Not seen in Lloyds 1802.

**Fanny Anne.** Built at Newport 1801. Sloop. 22 ton. 37 feet long. In Cardigan Register 1801 no.13 and Cardigan 1835 no. 93. Lost off Milford Haven 27th May 1841.

**Jupiter.** Built at Newport 1802. Sloop. 64 ton. In Cardigan Register 1802 no.83. 1826 no 27. 1834 no. 103. In 1805 Lloyds as J.Bowen master and owner. Not recorded in Lloyds in 1812. In Lloyds Register 1831, Smack, Built at Newport, 29 years previously. B.Bowen, master, Havard ownership. Single deck. Repairs done to vessel in 1821 and 1824, 64 ton. Seen in 1837 Lloyds as **Jupiter** built Newport in 1802, Sloop, 64 tons with master J.Davis and Havard as owner. It says port of Newport, which is a mistake as it would be Cardigan! Operating London to Bristol. Lost 1843 but not known where. As owned by the Havards assume built by them as well. Curiously there was a French ship and built in France called **Francois** also captained by a Havard in 1831.

**Lord Nelson**. Built at Newport 1802. Snow, 109 tons. In Cardigan Register 1802 no.34. Milford Register 1830 no.1. 1839 no.18. In Lloyds Register 1812 as a Brig built 1802 in Wales with 109 ton with Warlow as master and part owner. London to Heligoland and classified E1. There was a previous **Lord Nelson** built at Newport in 1782 Lost in 1840. I have failed to find where this **Lord Nelson** was lost but one amusing incident occurred in November 1823. Lord Nelson ,master Nicholas, was about to depart Dublin with provisions for London. It is not clear if she was at anchor or laying off. While some of the crew were taking the pilot ashore in the ship's boat, the brig was driven out to sea in a heavy gale. The **Lord Nelson** with only three persons aboard sailed to Fishguard where they arrived the next day. The remainder of the crew (perhaps 5 men) having been left behind in Dublin.

**Princess Royal.** Built at Newport 1803. Brigantine. 95 tons. In Cardigan Register 1803 no.30. In Lloyds 1836 as Princess Royal as Brig 96 ton built at Newport 1803, T.Jenkins master and D.Lloyd owner. Milford Registered. London to Liverpool trading. 96 tons in 1853. L.James master and James and Co. Owners in 1853. Fate unknown. Not to be confused with 33 ton sloop lost in March 1824 which was built Llansaintfraed in 1806.

**Charlotte.** Built at Newport 1804. Schooner. 86 ton (82 /74 /104 tons) . In Cardigan Register 1804 no.38 . 1825 no.74. 1846 no. 6. In Lloyds 1820 and 1826 as 86 tons built in Wales 1804 Williams master, Lloyd and Co .owners. In Lloyds Register in 1836 as **Charlotte,** 82 ton Schooner built Newport 1804, Williams master and owner. A new deck was put on her in 1832. In 1836 she traded London to Dublin, classified AE1. In 1854 Lloyds she has gone over to Wexford with J Sheil as master owner and her tonnage increased to 104 tons, built 1804, Newport. Assume Lloyds built. As this was the second vessel built at Newport with this name, I surmise that the **Charlotte** of Newport built in 1798 may have been lost about 1803.

**Culloden of Newport.** Built at Newport 1804. Schooner. 83 tons. In Cardigan Register 1805 no.1 Cardigan 1816 no 12. Cardigan 1825 no.71. Lloyds of 1808 and 1810 has a **Culloden** sloop 55 tons built in Wales in 1804, captain and owner J.Davies, surveyed in Dublin. In Lloyds Register for 1836 as **Culloden**, Brig built Newport in 1804 master J.Davies and owners Evans and Co. Cardigan register. Milford 1838 no.10. Milford 1852 no 6. She was lost Shields 25th June 1856 together with her crew. James Davies , master, is remembered on a gravestone in St Mary's Church. *(Seen Maritime Wales No.11 page 17)*

**Hope**. Built at Newport 1805. Sloop. 21 ton In Cardigan Register 1805 no.18 . Cardigan 1817 no.1. Cardigan 1825 no 112. Built by John Havard and Son. Lost at Goultrop Roads, near Little Haven 5thMarch 1827. The ship was wrecked in St. Bride's Bay. Her crew were rescued. She was on a voyage from Pembroke to Newport or vice versa . In Lloyds List 13 March 1827. The sloop **Hope,** of and from Newport (Pembrokeshire), Isaac, master, for Pembroke with roofing slates, oats, and coals, has been driven into Goltop Roads, in St. Bride's Bay, where she has been wrecked." Extract from Cambrian newspaper 10th March 1827.. 6,202. 13.03.1827 .
Goultrop Roads was a favourite anchorage for vessels going north from Milford Haven. Vessels could reach there on one tide when leaving Milford Haven. However, many sloops and schooners were lost there when trapped by a Northerly or North-Easterly wind. The seabed of the anchorage is littered with slates and granite blocks (road sets), from the cargoes of lost sailing ships.

**Neptune.** Built at Newport 1805. Sloop. 70 ton In Cardigan Register 1806 no.4.   1805 Lloyds has Brig of 84 tons built Newport 1797 master Humphries and owners Capt &Co.  In 1810 as **Neptune** sloop 70 ton built in Wales in 1806 . Captain and owner . J. Griffith . Dublin and Cork trading.  Lloyds 1830 has a 58 ton sloop built Wales in 1810 with Kehoe master and Devereaux owners.

**Fanny & Mary**. Built at Newport 1807. Sloop. 32 ton In Cardigan Register 1807 no.32. Not seen in Lloyds 1808-1810

**Valiant** Built at Newport in 1812 Brig 144 tons., Master Owen of Newport when the vessel was lost in 1825. The Cambrian Newspaper tells us that this vessel came ashore onto Goodwick Sands in a gale before the 1st December 1825. "The **Valiant**, master Owen of Newport, laden with iron ore etc ran on shore on Goodwick Sands." A further report says that she was from Barrow with iron ore destined for Newport, Monmouthshire, when she (like two other ships) was driven from her anchors and came ashore and was totally wrecked, crew saved. *North Wales Gazette 1st December 1825 p.3*

This ink sketch (owned by the author) is the Snow **Heart of Oak of Cardigan** 148 tons, built at Poole in 1792. She is depicted in a "Gale of Wind" in the Bay of Biscay on 23rd October 1823. She was eventually lost in Bridlington Bay in March 1848, fortunately her crew of six saved themselves.

**Mary Anne.** Built at Newport 1810. Sloop. 28 ton In Cardigan Register 1810 no.8, Cardigan 1826 no.19. A memorial stone at St Mary's Church is to Captain William Mathias aged 32 who died 30th September 1812. He was the first master of the **Mary Anne.** In 1826 Captain Thomas Evans, was her captain with the greatest ownership (16/64ths). She was built by William Lloyd in Newport yet John Havard, shipwright, had 8/64 ownership of the vessel. Details of the vessel say that she had no figurehead, 1 deck, 1 mast, that her mast length from the inner part of the main stem to the forepart of the stern aloft is 39.3 feet, her breadth midships is 12 feet, her depth in hold at midships is 6.4 feet. Sloop rigged with a standing bowsprit, square stern, carvel built. *(www.peoplescollection.wales/items/45145)*

In the great gale of 26 October 1859 she came ashore like others at Traeth-gwyn, New Quay, Ceredigion. "Below Fron- Wig, the **Pearl** recently repaired, was lying on its side against the rocks being battered by waves; the **Mary Hughes,** the **Perseverence** and the **Margaret and Anne** were crashing together and being completely submerged at times by the huge seas. Behind Penpolion, the **Mary Eliza** had sunk completely and the **Elle** was on the rocks. The **Mary Anne**, the smack **Margaret** and the **Major Nannery** were driven ashore at Traeth-gwyn. At time of the gale, the **Mary Anne** was owned by a consortium all from Newport, Pembrokeshire - Thomas Evans of Newport, mariner (16 shares), John Havard of Newport, shipwright (8 shares), David Williams of Newport, mariner (24 shares), David Evans of Rhosymaen, Newport, merchant (8 shares), Elizabeth Thomas of Newport, widow (8 shares), and Anne Nicholas of Newport, widow (8 shares).

The Customs log book entry for the **Mary Anne,** quite clearly shows her as being built in Newport in 1810.

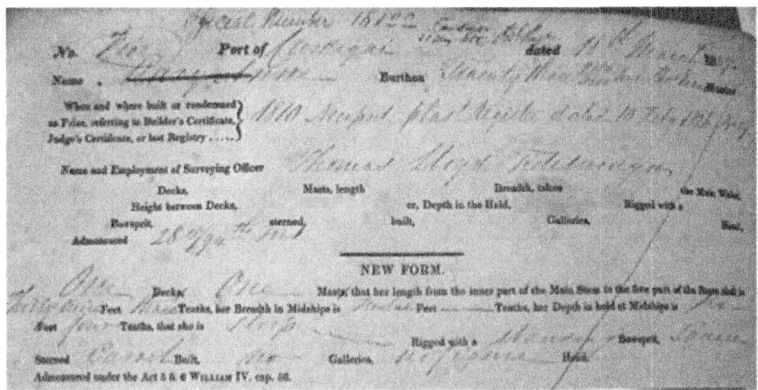

Photograph © Pembrokeshire Archives, Haverfordwest.

The newspapers of the day confirm that she was completely lost at New Quay, Cardigan on the 25-26th October 1859. Her crew fortunately were rescued. This is the same gale that caused the **Mathildis** to be lost at Cwm yr Eglwys when her entire crew was lost.

The sloop's registration documentation notes that the **Mary Anne** had been broken up before 1866. The Peoples Collection Wales asks the question, did the **Mary Anne** break up in 1859 or did she trade for a few more years until 1866? To find an answer we see if she is listed in a Lloyds Register between those years. In 1856 to 61 Lloyds Register there is no **Mary Anne** although plenty of **Mary Ann** and **Mary Anne** including one 22 ton Smack built in New Quay in 1825 with a master W.James. Thus as she was not listed with Lloyds immediately before 1859 we cannot determine from these records if the loss date of the 1859 gale applies to the same vessel.

I had a closer look at all the 1859 newspapers regarding the losses reported around the coast . *The Pembrokeshire Herald and General Advertiser* for the date 11th November 1859 gives a list of all vessels **totally lost** in the gale together with lives lost.
*...all saved Major Nanney, at Newquay, all saved Mary Jane, at Newquay, all saved Mary Ann, at Newquay, all saved Morning Star, at Cardigan, all drowned Martha Jane, …..*

This conveniently confirms that **Mary Ann** was totally wrecked yet thankfully all the crew were saved. This would make sense as with any serious damage this Sloop would not be worth saving. She was built in 1810 and she had survived well for 49 years. There were many newer vessels to salvage after the October 1859 gale, which caused no less than 800 lives to be lost.

**Victory of Newport** . Built at Newport 1811. Brigantine of 120 tons /118 tons In Cardigan Register 1811 no.10 and again seen in Cardigan Register 1825 no. 4. We know her master died on 9th January 1819 which is the same date as the Brig **Victory** was wrecked near Fishguard, Pembrokeshire with the loss of all hands.

**Minerva** . Built at Newport 1811. Brig 102 tons. . Havard owned and probably Havard built. See **Minerva** later under Newport owned vessels. There was a Sloop, **Minerva** built in Cardigan in 1814, owned by David Davies .

**Hope of Fishguard** . Built at Newport 1812. Sloop 29 ton. In Cardigan Register 1813 no.4 also 1826 no.71 and 1840 no.1. Recorded as lost off Padstow 1843. Seen in Lloyds 1832 as Hope built at Newport in 1814. A 29 ton Sloop with master R,Rees, owners Beynon & Co. In Cardigan Register in 1832. Out of Lloyds register in 1845 so the year of loss could be 1843.

**David of Cardigan** . Built at Newport 1813. Sloop, 35 ton. Owned by David Davies of Cardigan. Lost 1849 no other information . Not to be confused with the **David**, the 26 ton Sloop built 1830 that was lost in Ramsey Sound in 1882.

**Mary Ann** Built at Newport 1816, Sloop, 23 ton. Built by William Lloyd. In 1814 there was a Mary Ann Lloyd, a widow of a sea captain, it is likely that this Sloop was named after her. I surmise that another shareholder would be Geo. Lloyd a gent living at Woodstock . This vessel was eventually lost in May 1906 at Abermawr Beach, near Mathry. Crew saved. Her timbers were salvaged for construction at Tregwynt Woollen Mill. See story of loss of **Mary Ann** .

**Artuose of Newport.** Built at Newport 1814. Brig. 157 ton. In Cardigan Register 1814 no. 15. Milford 1837 no. 15. In Lloyds Register of 1836 as Brig 150 ton built by William Lloyd in Newport (son of Thomas Lloyd). Her captain from the launch was John Wade of Fishguard, Classified as E1. In March 1848 there was still a Wade as master, so we can assume either an old John Wade or his son had taken over command. Papers and receipts of the **Artuose** are in the Havard papers at the National Library of Wales. See later. In 1863 she carried a crew of 10 men. She was wrecked on Cardiff Flats on 8th March 1876. Not to be confused with a schooner same name built in Cardigan in 1823.

**Diligence** Built at Newport in 1814. Brig. 100 tons. In 1831 Lloyds she is still afloat with Jones as master and Lewis & co as owners. I have not confirmed if it is the same vessel but a **Diligence** went ashore and assumed wrecked on Spike Island near Youghal in 1840. She was on a voyage from Llanelly to Courtmacsherry, Courtmac is 30 miles SW of Cork. (*www.irishwrecksonline.net/Lists/CorkListG.htm*)

**Eliza**. Built at Newport 1814. Brig. 147 ton. In Cardigan Register 1814 no. 14. 1825 no.3. 1837 no. 16. This **Eliza** was lost at Mumbles Head on 3rd January 1854, Mumbles Head. She was in ballast from Waterford and anchored off Swansea when a SE force 10 storm drove her from her anchors onto Mumbles Head. All the crew (7 men) saved themselves in their own ship's boats. Brig totally wrecked and was insured at £200. The ship was aged 41 years old when lost with all her papers. Ten years before in 1844 she sailed from Milford to Waterford with Frederick Seaborne as master. He was master from 1829, and a memorial stone is seen in St Mary's Church, he died 1851 aged 62. In 1853 J. Seaborne (assume his son) was captain.

**Venerable of Newport.** Built at Newport 1815. Brigantine. 127 ton./130 ton. In Cardigan Register 1815 no. 22. In Lloyds 1820-1826 as Venerable Brig built Newport 1815, 127 ton master J. George and owners Harris & Co. The Harries mentioned as owners are likely to include James Harries of Dinas, Thomas Harries of Cefn Hendre and David Harries, a mariner, living in Fishguard. In 1827 her master changed from J.George to J.Phillips. This vessel is missing from the Lloyds in 1829 so she is likely wrecked in 1828 but I have found no record of her loss.

**Wreckers at Newport.** On 18th January 1819 there was a large Liverpool ship named **Venerable.** A 400 ton Brig that ended up coming ashore at Newport with a cargo of palm oil and ivory from Africa to Liverpool. She may have had some slaves on board as well. All the crew of 30 and some of the cargo was saved. She was 15 weeks out from West Africa and her captains first sight of land was Strumble Head, a few hours later his command was a total wreck. Three local magistrates who, spending all the first night on the beach prevented the ship being plundered by the "…inhuman wreckers who infest that coast". This is the only reference I have seen to the word *wreckers* being used in the Newport area.

This is a pen and ink drawing of the **Ant,** a Newport built ship passing the Smalls Lighthouse. This is the original lighthouse, 51.721239°N 5.669831°W, a wooden structure on oak pillars put there in 1776 and lasted until the existing granite lighthouse was lit in 1861. The picture is detailed enough to see that **Ant** is rigged as a Snow, but looks at a distance like a Brig with an added fore and aft mainsail. This vessel was built by Levi Havard in 1816, with owners from both Newport and St Dogmaels. She was lost in 1832.

At 136 tons **Ant** was one of the larger vessels built on the banks of the River Nevern. She has a square transom with stern carving and carries a small boat on davits . She would not carry any guns but was painted to show gun ports. This was to confuse French privateers that were capturing British vessels in the Channel at the time. Just two years before she was launched another Havard ship had in fact been captured and held ransom by the French. It must have prompted Levi Havard to paint this ship with gun ports. He may have even started the trend which was common on merchant vessels from 1820 to 1870 . *Image: Tom Bennett collection.*

**Ant**. Built at Newport 1816. Snow. 136 and 126 ton In Cardigan Register 1816 no.9. 1825 no. 22. In Lloyds Register 1820 and 1831 no 1056, Brig rig , One deck. Master David Owen, owners Owens, built 1816 at Newport. Classified A1 voyages Liverpool to Limerick in 1820, by 1831 her Classification dropped to E1. David Owens her original master lived in St Dogmaels, where other shareholders lived. In Lloyds 1830 the **Ant** is listed with D.Owens still as master and Brig rigged, Official number 1060. 125 tons, Newport built in 1816, classified as E at a survey in Plymouth. No repairs done to her.

See pen and ink drawing of this ship passing the original wooden Smalls lighthouse. My original records say lost in 1832, but I can find no more details of her loss. There was a sailing ship **Ant** lost 18th September 1821 with copper ore from Cardiff lost off St David's Head. Crew saved in their own boat and landed at Milford. Another **Ant** this time a Sloop was lost of the Smalls on 5th September 1830. Not to be confused with another **Ant** a Brigantine built 1810 of 84 tons (Swansea Register) that was lost on a voyage Memel, Germany to Neath in 1827. Not in Lloyds in 1839.

**Ardent.** Built at Newport 1817. Snow. 125 ton. In Cardigan Register 1817 no. 3. 1826 no. 46. 1836 no. 3. As there was a previous **Ardent** built at Newport in 1800, it can be supposed that this second ship was built a year after the previous one was lost. Seen in Lloyds Register of 1845 and 1857 as Brig of Cardigan 138 tons with Captain Joseph Dodding. Lost off Shetlands 11th January 1858. She is no longer seen in Lloyds in 1858 which seems to confirm this loss date. Ignore the entry in Larn's Database as lost at Llansaintffraid in December 1858 as that is incorrect.

**Friendship.** Built at Newport 1817. Brig. 83 ton. In Cardigan Register. Owned by David Davies of Ship Hotel, Cardigan. In Lloyds Reg 1836 **Friendship** Brig 93 tons of Cardigan 1817, D Davies master and Davies & Co. as owners . On 9th November 1819 a **Friendship,** Kinsale to Swansea sank off The Smalls, crew saved.

**Mary of Newport.** Built (or rebuilt) at Newport 1819 Sloop. 53 ton. In Cardigan Register 1819 no 10. 1825 no.41. Seen in Lloyds Ship Register dated 1827-1830, Sloop, 52 tons, built at Newport in 1819. Master L.Davis with owners Davis & Co. Class A1. She was last surveyed in Topsham and had started using iron cables on her anchors. A Newport **Mary** got into difficulties on 19th December 1853. Driven from her anchors in wind conditions ENE 10, This smack **Mary** struck a rock in Jack Sound and went to pieces. With a crew of 4 she was sailing from Newport to Pembroke Dock. The crew were saved by a boat that put out from Marloes. *(Larn Shipwreck Database 2000.).*

**Hope** Brig 182 ton built Newport in 1823 Cardigan register. Seen as having J Havard as master in 1837, so assume Havard built. Lloyds 1837 has no other details. Seen again in 1845 and 1862 Lloyds as Brig **Hope** built Newport 1823, master T. Williams. Owners Evans & Co. This is the first Newport vessel seen that I have seen trading with Mediterranean and still from the port of Cardigan.

**Lady Day of Fishguard.** Built at Newport or Milford 1825. Schooner. 128 ton. Newport owners. Seen in Lloyds Register 1827 as 130 ton Schooner built in Newport in 1825. Her last survey was done in London and she carried iron chain cables, denoted by the abbreviation PIC (proved Iron cables) The abbreviation of PIC is entered for the first time on two Newport vessels around 1827. The **Mary**, of similar tonnage had also started to use chain instead of rope for anchor cables. Such information becomes important when trying to identify a wrecksite. As chain can be looked for near a winch and the shape of the anchor ring may change. Lloyds List 1834. Master was lost 5th February 1837 in Cardiff, and perhaps this vessel was lost the same day.

**Swift of Newport.** Built at Newport 1825. Sloop. 39 ton. In Cardigan Register 1825 no 83. In Lloyds Register 1837 and 1846 with J.Mathias as master and Mathias and Co as owners, Sloop. 39 ton built 1825 Cardigan..I have discovered the loss years of a few **Swift** but they do not appear to be the correct vessel. In 1834 a **Swift** was lost off Formby, with entire crew and vessel lost. I have seen a note that the Newport one was lost 1837, but that must be the wrong date as she was afloat 9 years later. On 3$^{rd}$ January 1839 there was a **Swift** that struck rocks and sank at Newton-by- the-Sea, Northumberland. Her crew survived. There was also a smack **Swift** that was run down off the Skerries in February 1841.

**Eliza** Built at Newport 1826 Brig 102 ton In Lloyds in 1829 giving master J.Williams and then added later W.Lewis as master with Williams & Co, owners trading Dublin to Petersburg. (St.Peterburg). Her master died in October 1851 but the ship continues. Entered in Lloyds Register of 1862 as **Eliza** 97 ton Brigantine built Cardigan 1827. Master T.Lewis and owners Owens & Co. In 1857 the same vessel is marked as a schooner in Lloyds but all subsequent entries list her as a 97 ton Brigantine. She is missing from Lloyds registration in 1870.

**Elizabeth of Newport.** Built at Newport 1826. Schooner. 108 ton.
In Cardigan Register 1826 no 37. Milford Register 1836 no.5. . In Lloyds 1829 with master W.Lewis and owners Lewis & Co. Classified A and traded Wales to Bristol. In 1854 Schooner 85 ton with J Evans as master owners still Lewis & Co. Milford registered said to change to Plymouth Register 1859.

On 23rd March 1866 the smack **Elizabeth** of Cardigan, under the command of Captain T. Mathias, was lost on Cardigan Bar. This was the Smack built at Cardigan in 1844 of 36 ton and not the large schooner built at Newport. . The Nautical Magazine and Naval Chronicle for 1867 says that 6 persons were saved from the smack **Elizabeth of Cardigan** which then was wrecked, it fails to say if it is the same incident.

**Providence**   Built at Newport 1826. Sloop. 28 ton. Assume Cardigan Register 1826.   Not in Lloyds in 1845.

**Hope.**   Built at Newport 1826  Snow. 112 ton. Assume Havard built. In Lloyds Register in 1834 giving J.Havard as master and registered at Cardigan. My original records had  **Hope.**  Built at Newport 1823. Snow. 112 ton.

**Hope**   Built either Cardigan or at Newport in 1826  A large Smack of 71 tons  seen in Lloyds Register in 1845 master R.Owens  owner J.Griffiths recorded as Built at Cardigan 1826.

**Hope**.  Built at Newport 1827. Snow, 182 ton.  In Lloyds Register in 1833 as being built in Newport in 1832 and registered as a Brig 182 ton with D. Nicholls as captain and Nichols & Co. as owners.  What I find interesting is that on its first survey it was given an AE1 category for 36 years. This was the largest ship built by the Havards.

**Betsey.** Built at Newport 1827. Sloop. 24 ton.  Not sure if this is correct as I can find no record of a **Betsey** built on this date in Newport.  The Cardigan Register of 1827 needs to be consulted to confirm . Not in Lloyds in 1837 or 1845.

**Brothers.**  Built at Newport 1828. Schooner. 99 ton. In Cardigan Register 1828 no 5. Cardigan 1837 no 2. Milford 1845 no. 6 .  Master D. Evans died 1834. D. Evans owner and master.  D. Evans (son?) master in 1836 when trading Cardiff to Sligo. Classified A1.   Seen in Lloyds 1837 as master D.Evans and owners Capt & Co. Still at home port of Cardigan.  Lost 1856.  A Schooner of Swansea of this name, 66 tons, was lost in Ireland in 1854, she broke from moorings in Ballydonegan.

**Grace of Fishguard.** Built at Newport 1828. Schooner. 103 ton. In Cardigan Register 1828 no 2. Milford Register 1828 no. 27 and 1841 no.3. Seen in 1829 Lloyds as **Grace,** Schooner 103 ton built year before at Newport. W. Jenkins as master. D. Evans & Co. as owners. My notes says she had Fishguard owners which is why she was registered in Milford. Given A1 for 11 years! Seen in 1837 Lloyds, same vessel same master but 104 tons. Seen in Lloyds 1845 in Milford registry giving built at Newport in 1828, Schooner 104 tons with captain as T.Morgan and Hutchings & Co as owners. Lloyds Register of 1865 -1868 gives details and her dimensions of 64.3 feet long by 19.6 feet beam with 10.3 feet draft. Repairs were carried out in 1861. Master now W.Jones and owners Morgan &Co. Milford registered. Missing in Lloyds 1874 so assume lost between 1868 and 1874. Fate Unknown.
Not to be confused with a St Ives Schooner **Grace** of 74 ton that went missing in St Georges Channel (Irish Sea) in 1862, Liverpool to Dundalk, nothing heard of vessel or crew from that Date.

**Elizabeth Anne** Built at Newport in 1835. Schooner 109 tons in 1842 went to Aberystwyth registry 18/1842. The **Elizabeth Anne** was sold as a wreck at Penzanze in March 1871.

**Harmony.** Built at Newport 1829. Schooner. 95 ton. In Cardigan Register 1829 no 16. Cardigan 1838 no.6. Milford 1854. In the Lloyds Register 1831 her captain was William Havard . Sailing Welsh coast and Dublin 1830-1835. In Lloyds in 1845 as Schooner of Cardigan 70 ton, D.Griffiths as captain. In Lloyds 1850, captain now J. Griffiths . Griffiths may have taken over **Harmony** when William Havard became captain of the large brig **Anne** in 1842. Lloyds 1874-5 gives a Cardigan schooner **Harmony** 70 tons built at Cardigan (although we know it means Newport) in 1829 with Havard and Co as owners with W.Williams as master. Dimensions are also given as 59.0 feet long by 17.0 ft beam by 10.6 ft depth. Missing from Lloyds Register in 1883. Fate Unknown.The Lloyds Register 1874 also has another schooner **Harmony** saying built Newport in 1836. However because it has the name Young as a builder we know this to be John Young, shipbuilder in Newport Monmouthshire.

**Maria and Anne**. Built at Newport 1830. Owned by David Davies and Banc y Llong, Aberystwyth. In Lloyds Register of 1837 as 65 ton sloop built at New Quay in 1830, master E.Evans with owners Capt &Co. Registered at Cardigan. Valued at £1,200 for estate of Thomas David's father David Davies, around 1840.

**David**  Built at Newport 1830. Smack  26 ton. In Cardigan Register 1830 no.19s. Captain David Davies.  Cardigan Register 1837 no. 31. Captain Thomas Lewis of St Dogmaels in 1837-1847.  It was not listed in 1835 Lloyds Register but was in the Lloyds Register again in 1847.  It is entered in Lloyds 1854 with s T.Edwards, master and D.Davies as owner and still 26 ton Smack. The name 'David' may be influenced by the owners name David Davies of Cardigan.  Sank and lost in the middle of Ramsey Sound 16th December 1882 in wind conditions SSE force 7. Master Edwards of St Dogmaels, with another 2 crew all saved but the vessel sank. Carrying a cargo of culm (anthracite dust and limestone mix), she was on a voyage from Milford to Newport, Pembrokeshire.  In Lloyds 1874-5  her dimensions are given as 40.0 feet long by 12.5 ft beam and 7.0 ft depth. T. Edwards master and Edwards & Co as owners. Built 1830 Newport. Official No. 10276. The ship's papers (certificates) went down with the ship, indicating the crew had to abandon in a hurry. Diver Greg Evans, together with Martin and Louise Coleman have studied a wooden wreck lying at a depth of 27m in Ramsey Sound. Its dimensions and dates fit the identity of the **David.**

This dark glass prism light from the wreck is especially significant as I think it shows that the Havards were the first to place such deck lights in culm sloops. They are to observe if the coal has caught fire below deck, without opening hatches.

**Frances**  Built at Newport or Cardigan in 1830. Schooner 71 tons. Lloyds 1845 has a Schooner 47 ton of Cardigan built Cardigan 1830 with Davies as master.  Seen in Lloyds 1852 with master as T. Davies and classed as A1 from a Lloyds survey in Cardigan in 1851.  Fate unknown.

*This photograph is of the schooner* **Ellen Beatrice.**

She was a topsail schooner built in 1865, 88 tons, 73.5 feet length. She was not built in Newport but is very similar to ***Phoebe*** that was built in Newport. The schooner is drying her sails in Aberystwyth Harbour; probably about 1890.

In such early photographs the exposure time was usually over one minute. The photographer has to tell anyone in the shot to not move otherwise the image will not be distinct but a smudged looking outline. There is a boatman in a small boat near the bows of the schooner who is trying hard not to move his sculling oar. He looks like a ferryman rather than one of the crew and is probably the man who took the photographer out into the harbour to take the photograph.

**Reform.** Built at Newport 1831 Sloop 14 ton. In Cardigan Register 1831 no 9. Not seen in Lloyds 1845.

**Ocean.** Built at Newport 1832. Brig. 121 ton.(106 tons ) In Cardigan Register 1832 no 4. 1836 no. 6. Later of 106 tons, with owner David Davies. Moved to Llanelly 1854. In 1832 and 1836 her master was Captain David Nicholas of Cardigan, trading between London and Dublin in 1836 (121 tons). In 1855 she was in Llanelly Register with her captain and owner as E.Bentley. Brig of 121 tons. Built Newport 1832. Her rig was changed to a schooner. Around 1840 the Brig **Ocean** was valued at £1,893 estate duties for Thomas David's father. The **Ocean** finally came to the end of her life in an October gale in 1861. The London Illustrated News reports the loss of the ship , "The schooner **Ocean** of Llanelly, Captain Edwin Bentley, was observed to be about three miles south west of Newhaven in distress. Her headsails were gone and they were obliged to run before the wind. She attempted to enter the harbour. But as there was insufficient water, she drifted into the bay at the back of the pier. This occurred about seven o'clock and soon after daybreak as she struck, two boats were immediately sent out to rescue the crew. The sea was running mountains high .. But the men rowed like heroes. The first boat getting to the distressed ship took off three crew, the second boat close behind took off the captain the mate and the remainder of the crew with all their clothing and effects. Leaving the vessel at a time when there was not the remote hope of saving her. The crew were taken to the Coastguard Station where every attention was paid to their wants. The Ocean soon became a total wreck". *The Illustrated London News - Volume 22 - Page 379,* Loss date 8th October 1861. The 14 men who rowed out to save the crew were each awarded 5 Shillings by the National Lifeboat Institution, equivalent to about two days wages.

**Agnes**. Built at Newport 1833. Schooner. 89 ton. I found this vessel in Lloyds Register of 1837 where it says built Newport 1832, This could be Newport Mon, but I do not think so. Her captain did not have a Welsh name and she had moved to Portsmouth, captain FdeGaris and trading to Guernsey. Not in Lloyds in 1852 and not the schooner of this name that foundered off Grassholm in June 1852.

**Ann & Betsey.** Built at Newport (unspecified) 1833. Smack 22 ton. Glen Johnson says transferred to Cardigan Register, so it may have been built in Newport Mon. Not seen in Lloyds 1832. Vessel scrapped in 1920.

**Jane** Built in Newport in 1837, a schooner of 78 tons that was in the Cardigan Registry 1837 no.70. **Jane** United Kingdom 7th February 1838. The ship was driven ashore west of Calais, France. She was on a voyage from Newcastle upon Tyne, Northumberland to Calais. She was later refloated and taken into Calais. This maybe the same occasion, lost in 1838 on a voyage from London to Galway. John Morris of Newport, born c 1815, perished at sea between Galway and London in 1838, on the Schooner **Jane**. All crew were lost.
It would seem that as soon as this vessel was lost, another one was built, but this time in Cardigan. This subsequent **Jane** listed in the 1840 Lloyds, a **Jane** built in Cardigan in 1838 of 98 ton with J.James as master and James & Co, as owners. However the 1854 Lloyds also gives a **Jane,** schooner of 98 tons that says Cardigan built in 1834 and has J.James as master and owner but is not classified. Lloyds in 1874 has **Jane,** Built 1838, 98 ton in Cardigan with a T.Morgan as captain. *The Aberystwyth Observer dated 8th March 1879 News page 4* states ;*Glasgow Herald, Saturday, March 1, 1879* "The schooner **Jane** of Cardigan with a cargo of coal, is on shore quarter of a mile west of Kilcredaun Lighthouse, and is likely to become a total wreck. Crew saved." Kilcredane is in Shannon Estuary County Clare on the west coast of Ireland, a long way from Newport. Her Official No. 25278 Dimensions: 66 feet long, 20.3 ft beam and 11.6 ft draft. Her captain was T.Morgan. Ran aground in Position. 52.34 N / 09.43 W. Owner James and Co. Her Official Number 25278. Built 1838 in Cardigan.

**Agenoria.** Built at Newport 1834. Schooner. 117 ton. In Cardigan Register 1834 no.4 &17. 1837 no.9 .1834 Captain William Evans. Who lived at Ty'r Major, Newport was her master for more than 20 years. She maintained her Lloyds A1 classification throughout her life of 43 years. In June 1842 she sailed from Nantes to Newport, Mon. In April 1844 the '**Agenoria**' sailed from Barrow to Cardiff, in May from Milford to Cardiff, and in June from Cardiff to Dantzig. In May 1846 she sailed from London to Llanelli. Captain Evans seems to have relinquished the vessel soon afterwards, He died aged 49 in April 1868. From 1852 to 1854 her master was Benjamin Lodwick (Lodwig). Glen Johnson notes that her rig was changed to a Brigantine in 1852, and certainly in 1855 Lloyds has that designation. However it appears that when John Davis became master he changed her rig back to the original schooner rig as in 1874 she was a schooner with the same 117 tons. An **Agenoria** of Bideford was wrecked at Tenby 20th December 1855 involving RNLI awards for the rescue of two of her crew. Another **Agenoria** of Aberystwyth foundered off Anglesey on 29th July 1879, also with a coal cargo and the crew saved. Neither of these being the older **Agenoria** built at Newport. The Newport built **Agenoria** is still in the Lloyds Register of 1874 and her dimensions are given 173.3 feet long by 36.7 ft beam by 11.2 ft depth. Still at 117 tons and in Cardigan. Master was J.Davies and her owners were Davies & Co. Schooner rigged. " On 28th March 1880 the ship was lost, though the crew were saved." Location of loss not known.

**Alert.** Built at Newport 1835. Sloop 33 ton. In Cardigan Register 1835 no. 6. 1837 no. 5. Not seen in Lloyds 1874. Lost at St David's Head 3rd February 1881.

**Claudia of Newport.** Built at Newport 1835. Schooner. 135 ton. In Cardigan Register 1835 no. 21. 1836 no. 43. Havard built. In October 1835 one of her first trips was from Newport to Ostend. Lloyds Register of 1837 only has one **Claudia** mentioned. A schooner of 103 tons Built at Newport 1835 with J. Havard as master and the Havard & Co. as owners

John Havard was captain of **Claudia** until 1849 when he died. David Richards of Borth (1835 -1866) as a boy of 15 years of age did his apprenticeship on the **Claudia** and the **Hopewell.** The ship continues and in Lloyds Register 1850-1854 still 103 tons, D.Griffiths master, Havard owned. Still in Cardigan Registry. Repairs were done to her in 1847 and 1850. She may have had Williams as a captain in 1850-1851. In 1856 she was in Portmadog, one assumes to pick up a cargo of slates. A Newport gravestone . Memorial 498 gives a date of 22$^{nd}$ May 1871 suggesting this is when this schooner was lost with loss of life. However the local newspapers do not seem to record her fate although on the 6$^{th}$ June 1871 a passing ship saw a round sterned schooner aground on the Bishops close to South Bishop Lighthouse. Although this is around the same date I have not confirmed if this is the same schooner. In National Library of Wales is a box of Havard Papers. The box is full of all things to do with the Havard ships and includes the account books of the **Claudia** including the crew's wages. In the same box is a leather wallet belonging to John Havard, the one that he would have had with him on board the **Claudia** in 1849. This vessel not to be confused with an Aberyswyth smack of the same name that sank in the Great Gale of 1859.

**Perfect.** Built at Newport 1836. Schooner. 124 ton. In Lloyds Register of 1839 this vessel is recorded as **Perfect** a Schooner built in Newport in 1836 master Edwards with owners as Capt. & Co. Soon after being built she moved to Youghal Registry in Ireland. In 1860 she is still listed but not classified with T.Edwards still as her Master.

**Ann & Betsey.** Built at Newport 1837. Smack. 27 ton. In Cardigan Register 1837 no. 6. Scrapped in 1920. (83 yrs of age). The NLW in the Havard Papers have original share certificates of the sloop **Ann & Betsey.** Not to be confused with the Aberystwyth Smack of 26 ton that sank off Strumble Head in October 1880.

**Phoebe. (Phebe)** Built at Newport 1839 Schooner. 123 ton. In Cardigan Register 1839 no. 6. Classed A1 in Lloyds until she was lost on 3rd January 1843, off Aberdovey. David Havard was master (aged 41). He was lost with his ship *(Memorial stone 388, St Mary's Church).* Built with part iron bolts by the Havards and owned by them. In 1871 there was a Phoebe Havard, a widow living at the Eagle Inn in Cardigan, she was aged 64, and could have been his wife or owner of this schooner. She would have been aged 32, when the **Phoebe** was named and launched.

**Elizabeth.** Built at Newport 1839 Sloop. 27 ton In Cardigan Register? Lost 1874.

**Providence** Maybe built Newport 1841 Schooner 70 ton. In my notes which I have been unable to check, was a **Providence** built at this time. Looking through the Lloyds Register of 1852, there is a **Providence** in the Cardigan registry that is not included in Glen Johnson's list of St Dogmaels or Cardigan built vessels. The Lloyds entry says 71 ton Schooner master J.Owen built Wales in 1841 with owners Owens & Co.

A delightful photograph from 1910 of the sailing ketch **Wave** and the steamer **Harparee.** Horse and carts have already unloaded their cargoes. The two boys are posing proudly in their best clothes and holding their model boats for the cameraman Edwards.
*Photograph courtesy of Martin Lewis*

**Anne**  Built at Newport 1842  Brig  161 ton  built by Levi Havard. "On Thursday last, the 12th May 1842 a fine clipper brig named the **Anne** was launched from the building yard of Mr. Levi Havard, Newport, of the burthen of 200 tons, for the Mediterranean trade, classing 12 years A1. to be commanded by Captain William Havard, late of the schooner **Harmony** of that port, being the principal owner thereof "  seen in *The North Wales Chronicle and Advertiser for the Principality, 31$^{st}$ May 1842, page 2.*   This is probably the last vessel to be built by Levi Havard. She is listed in Lloyds in 1844-1845 and 1848- 1849 having been given 12 years A1 classing as expected on her launch. Her master is given as Havard and owners Havard & Co. Brig of 161 tons.  Repairs were done in 1848 and she is seen again in Lloyds  in 1852 , still as Cardigan her home port. same details with Havard as captain, destined voyage Milford. Sometime between 1848 and 1866 she had a change of Master to Thomas and she changed to Milford port . Lloyds 1866 give her dimensions as  78 feet long by 22.5 ft beam by 12.7 ft depth. There was another captain change to J.Wood as seen in Lloyds 1868-69 and 1872 with a tonnage change to 143 tons. . Lloyds we see that she has been surveyed again and given another A1 class rating. And a tonnage of 148 tons. Official Number 22725. She is out of Lloyds register by 1883 suggesting she was lost in the period 1873 to 1882.

When Levi Havard laid the keel for a new ship he was careful in keeping to the same tried and tested dimensions of the ones he had built before. He then knew that the draught of the ship would be less than 13 feet. That was the maximum draught for vessels entering Parrog over Newport sand bar on most high waters. This was one factor why the Havards kept to the same hull dimensions, knowing that it was not practical to build any deeper draught vessels, if they were to trade with the home port. After spending a few hours researching the **Anne** I finally came across her fate. She was lost off the Orkneys north of Scotland in a November gale in 1874.  By her owners calling her the **Anne of Milford**, made life a bit easier tracing the date of her demise.

There were two wrecks that day. One was the **Erin**, and the other the **Anne of Milford**. "the **Erin** (brig), of and for Liverpool, from Cronstadt, with deals and battens, struck on Skerry reefs here, during the hurricane of 30th November and became a total wreck: master Chenowith and cook drowned. Kirkwall, 22nd December 1874 "the sale of the stranded brig Erin, of Liverpool, took place at Deerness, on the 11th December : and that of the brig **Anne of Milford,** at Sunday, on the 17th both vessels being total wrecks: cargoes most part secured." *NMRS, MS/829/69 (no. 2552).*

The cargo of the **Anne of Milford** is not mentioned, but it can be assumed that both vessels had departed from Kronstadt, near Saint Petersburg, Russia, with a cargo of timber deals for Liverpool. The two ships were about the same tonnage and the captains would have known each other. Thus I think they departed the Russian port at the same time and ended up being wrecked in nearly the same place. It was a daring voyage for the two ships as had they remained in the arctic port for a few more weeks they may have been iced in. The wood cargo must have helped the two ships stay afloat during their ordeal preventing them from sinking and enabling them to be run ashore. The master of the **Erin** was washed overboard and drowned. Had they been carrying another cargo we could expect the entire crew of nine from each ship to be lost. The weather is always pretty hostile in the winter months in the North sea and the Newport crew were very lucky to survive this November ENE force 12.

When the loss dates are investigated I was surprised how many of these Newport ships were lost in the winter months. Many of the smaller trading vessels would cease trading in the winter, for fear of getting caught out in adverse weather.

This is a Brig rigged sailing ship taken by pioneer photographer Henry Fox Talbot in 1845. It is beached in Swansea and maybe having temporary repairs done to her. It is very similar to the Havard ships built at Newport. I have spent some time looking at this picture and although it is only a guess I think it could be **Anne** built at Newport in 1842, a Brig of 161 ton lost in 1874. There are a few pointers to make me believe it could be the **Anne.** Measuring various parts of the photograph, like the ladder and the thwarts in the small rowing boat, the deck length I reckon to be is 66 feet long . The **Anne** was 72 feet. My estimate could be 6 feet out. Other dimensions look similar. Not many ports in Wales built ships of this size in 1842, and Newport Pembrokeshire was one of the nearest doing so. Unless the masts have been touched up (no Photoshop then!) They do look very white, like a relatively new ship. The **Anne** was less than two years old at the time and the black and white painted gun ports were a classic hallmark of all Havard brigs after 1822. Some foreign ships would go to Swansea to get their hulls copper bottomed. However this was never done on the **Anne,** but she was repaired at Swansea in 1847 and the author thinks that this photograph is actually done in that year and not two years previously.

**Below is a list of vessels with Newport or Dinas shareholders but built elsewhere. (Alphabetical under name of vessel)**

**Aid**  36 ton, Smack built at Cardigan in 1829. Seen in Lloyds 1854, 1859 and 1866 as Cardigan smack of 25 tons built Cardigan 1829 with master D.Jenkins and owners Jenkins & Co. Dimensions; 38.1 feet long by 12.7 feet beam by 6.7 feet depth. Lost in Ramsey Sound 13th September 1869 on same day as **Ann & Catherine** also described in the newspaper at the time as a Newport vessel.

**Anna Maria** . 47 ton Schooner built at Aberdovey 1784. On a voyage from London to Barmouth this vessel was totally lost together with Captain Morris and his 2 crew. The vessel was lost near Milford Haven end of November 1795. Reference Lloyds List no. 2,779, 1st Dec 1795.

**Britannia**  19 ton Sloop built at Cei Bach, Ceredigion in 1776.

**Britannia**  35 ton Sloop. Built at Barmouth 1779.

**Cambria**  25 ton Sloop built at Abercastle 1793.

**Castle Malgwyn.**  Built or rebuilt at Cardigan in 1800. Owned by Newport owners. Sloop, 100 ton. Lost at Fishguard 19th February 1833. Master Lewis. A storm of tremendous proportions hit the Pembrokeshire coast that night, causing at least 12 ships to be wrecked and a total of more than 23 sailors drowned. Two of the wrecks occurred at Fishguard but fortunately no lives were lost. **Castle Malgwyn,** described as a large brig in the local newspaper, was sheltering near the pier at Lower Fishguard. The ferocious gale drove her from her anchors and she smashed to pieces on the rocks of Lampit Cove. Another Cardigan owned vessel **Eliza** was also driven out from her anchorage in Lower Fishguard, drove across the bay and hit rocks near Cow and Calf, where she sank.

**Commerce**. Sloop. 35 ton built at Carmarthen 1800. Sloop. 23ton owned Dinas/Newport built Conwy 1840.(?) This sloop was lost 2nd November 1873.

**Connium**  Sloop 23 ton, Newport owned but built elsewhere in 1840. Totally wrecked at Pwllgwaelod, Dinas Head 2nd November 1872.

**Darling** sloop, sank on a voyage Swansea to Newport 9th October 1821. Her master David Griffith (aged 32) of Newport died. (Gravestone details St Mary's Church) He would have been a shareholder in this sloop, but I have found no other details.

**Dinas.** Sloop 38 ton owned Dinas built at Abercastle in 1820. Not in Lloyds 1845.

**Dove .** Sloop. 36 ton Built in Aberystwyth 1783. Glen Johnson has a **Dove** a 28 ton Sloop Cardigan registered that was built in Cardigan in 1798. In 1826, her master was James James. This I think is a different vessel. A **Dove** was wrecked on the Great Orme, Llandudno on 18th January 1817 on a voyage Cork to Liverpool. There was a **Dove,** master Williams sailing Newport to Cork in January 1844. She was not seen in Lloyds Register in 1804 or 1845.

**Eliza**. Brig. 135 ton owned Dinas, built Foreign.

**Eliza** In Lloyds 1812 there is an **Eliza,** 147 ton built in Wales in 1800 with a Captain W.Davis and owner Davis and Co. This Brig was lost Tramere Bay, Ireland on 17th December 1856. This is the same year that a Captain Davies living at Danydre died and his body returned from Ireland to Newport for burial.

**Eliza** In Lloyds 1829 there is an **Eliza** built at Newport in 1825
**Eliza.** Built Berkeley, Gloucester in 1822. Sloop 16 ton owned Nevern
**Eliza** Official No. 23944. In December 1863 expenses were being being sought by an agent in Milford for the cost of returning the crew of the **Eliza of Cardigan** back to their homes. She was lost near the Small Lighthouse on 14 August 1863 and all her crew were saved.

**Excel.** Brig 213 ton built Milford 1854. Lloyds 1860 has her listed as a Brig of 222 tons built Milford 1853, with D.Nicholas as master and Nicholas as owners. Operating from London.

**Exley** Sloop 29 ton built Hull 1840. 47 feet long. Not seen in Lloyds in 1845. (See Voyages list for 1870). Master John Jones of Newport. My notes say Lost Pencaer, Strumble Head 3rd April 1871, but I also have a note that soon after she commences trading again!

**Expedition**. Sloop 35 ton built Kidwelly 1809. In 1810 Lloyds there is a sloop of this name 32 tons that said Cardigan built 1809. D.Griffiths as master and owner. Surveyed in Bristol. In Lloyds 1820 there is a sloop with D. Jones as master/owner built 1809 Cardigan 43 ton.
Not seen Lloyds in 1845. In February 1822 an **Expedition** was wrecked on Carmarthen Bar with general cargo from Bristol, but I think she was Bristol registered and a different vessel. "On Sunday night last, at half past ten, the sloop **Expedition,** Griffiths, master, was ran on board (hull was hit) near St. Gowan's, by the schooner **Waterloo,** of Wicklow, coming before the wind, which carried away her bowsprit and stove in her stem and tow. The Commander of the schooner promised to tow them into Milford, but did not so. The **Expedition** is very leaky, and is under repairs." This is extracted from *The Cambrian 12th August 1837*. Whether this was her fate I am not sure.

**Fly**. Smack 23 ton. This smack under the Cardigan Registry was built in 1840 and had an owner G Jenkins. My original notes on the **Fly** say that she was not built in Newport but a different port before 1810 and that she was owned by Richard Jackson of Newport. However we know that the Cardigan 1840 built smack traded for 33 years before sinking with all her crew. There is no **Fly** of this size in the Lloyds register of 1812 or 1837, but she is a small vessel and may not be registered with Lloyds. In the shipping news we see outward from port of Llanelly in July 1837 was a vessel **Fly,** with a master Bowen from Aberthaw with limestone. In the Bristol shipping news in January 1839 there was a **Fly**, master Williams from Newport. Both these would appear to be the Newport owned smack. She sank 24th April 1873 off the coast between Strumble Head and Fishguard Roads when swamped by a heavy sea in North North Easterly force 6. The smack was heavily laden with a culm cargo from Pembrey on her way home to Newport.

The **Fly** foundered in the big seas some 15 miles off Fishguard, all her three crew going down with the vessel. They were caught in a big northerly with nowhere to go. It prompted more calls for a breakwater to be built at Fishguard to make a Harbour of refuge for vessels that found themselves in such circumstances.

**Frances.** Sloop 33 ton . Aberporth 1808. There is a **Frances,** smack that sank at the Waterings in Ramsey Sound carrying a cargo of random slates on 5$^{th}$ January 1867. She was said to have anchored in a gale and was swamped in shallow water; 5 Meters depth. I have dived on this wrecksite and the slates do not look like Caernarfon slates and could be Cilgerran slates. Some of the bigger slate slabs, perhaps cut for doorsteps were removed in the 1980's. Cilgerran slates would have been a common cargo for a Newport owned smack.

**Hope** Brig 155 ton built at Swansea in 1813. This is a large ship to be owned by Newport traders. No more information. The name **Hope,** like those of **Mary, Betsey, Elizabeth** and **Providence** are difficult to follow as there were many ships in each port having the same names. What is more confusing is that a vessel named **Eliza** could be built in Newport but then be registered in Youghal in Ireland and her history from there on being difficult to trace.

### Sloop Elizabeth & Mary lost here

Carreg Onnen, used to be called Carreg Owen, near Strumble Head.

**Hopewell**  Sloop of 71 ton built 1826 (?) but not in Newport. There was a **Hopewell** lost offshore between St Ann's Head and St Govans Head 25th December 1833. Captain Meyrick that was seen to founder in a gale. A Shipping news from Swansea reported on the 4th January 1834 that " a Sloop, said to be the Hopewell, master Meyrick of Aberystwyth, from Newport (Mon) was seen to go down off St Gowan's Head in the late gale" She had a coal cargo from Newport (Mon) and going to Aberystwyth. In Lloyds 1831 register this vessel is recorded as a 61 ton Sloop built in Wales in 1808 with J.Meyrick as captain and Capt. & Co as owners. She was surveyed in Dublin in 1829. One of the owners must have been from Newport and acquired shares in 1826. Captain Meyrick and all the crew were lost. The weather was so atrocious that no other sailing ships in the vicinity could go to their help. In the same gale another ship foundered off Skokholm Island. This was reported in the Milford News of 29th December 1833 as " A vessel with two masts, of about 120 tons was seen to go down off Skokholm Island on the 25th. " As the crews of both disappeared it was difficult to identify the vessels that had vanished. The one seen foundering off Skokholm was probably a schooner also going north to Fishguard or North Wales. Her identity was never ascertained.

**Hopewell**  Sloop 18 ton. Built at New Quay 1810. 37.5 ft long. Owned by David, George and John James of Newport. In 1831 her master was Lewis and she arrived in Swansea carrying a slate cargo. Assumed to be slate from Cilgerran. In 1837 with Captain Davies she took a cargo of oats to Swansea. This sloop was lost at Fishguard on 14th August 1852, but her crew all saved by Lower Fishguard men including Lower Town Harbourmaster.
Her cargo of bricks from Chester were also saved.
She was wrecked just inside the rocks of the Fort outside Lower Fishguard. I was told the bricks were used to build a property on New Hill, Goodwick, possibly where The Laurels now stands. At extreme Low Water Springs you will still see the odd brick in the sand, in the cove just landward of the Fort promontory.

**Hopewell** Sloop 34 tons  Built Llangrannog 1826. In 1847 Transferred to Cardigan. 1847 Captain David Davies. 30/09/1870 Struck Horse Rock, Ramsey Sound & sank. Crew saved. This is the entry seen in Glen Johnson's list of Cardigan vessels, I am not sure if this also had Newport owners.

**Jane**  Sloop 32 tons. Built at Fishguard 1832 .Not seen in Lloyds 1846.

**Jane**  Schooner 78 tons Built Newport 1837, Sank August 1838 on voyage London to Galway, John Morris master, aged 23, lost same date.

**Jane & Catherine.**  Sloop 29 ton. Built at Conway 1837.  This sloop was wrecked on 16$^{th}$ September 1869 . "…during a heavy gale the smack **Jane and Catherine,** of Newport, Pembrokeshire, came ashore in Ramsey Sound, and is a total wreck. Crew saved, almost miraculously'. *(Seen 17$^{th}$ September 1869  The Pembrokeshire Herald).*

**Jane & Margaret** . Sloop 29 ton Llansanffraid 1859.

**John**  Sloop. 28 ton. Milford built or at Dinas 1828. In Lloyds Register 1832, a 30 ton Smack, built in Wales in 1828 with a master and owner as J.Lewis, trading Waterford to Milford. Assumed built and named for owner captain John Lewis. Cardigan registered in 1853. Lost 26$^{th}$ May 1867 in Fishguard Bay then owned by Thomas Lamb of Fishguard.

**John.**  Schooner 89 ton. Built at Bridgwater 1770. In January 1805 there was a **John**, master Owen, Liverpool to Kinsale that stranded on Cardigan Bar, not known if same vessel.   In Lloyds in 1831 there is a schooner says built in Wales in 1822, possibly rebuilt at Newport on this date, 90 ton with J.Roberts as Captain and owner.

A **John** in 19$^{th}$ January 1831, captain James, on a voyage with wheat and oats from Cardigan to Bristol she put into Milford where she got upon an anchor and sunk. The cargo has been got up.  *The Carmarthen Journal and South Wales Weekly Advertiser  21$^{st}$ January 1831.* It is difficult to know which **John** was involved but it seems that the vessel was repaired and continued to sail after 1833.

Looking through early photographs of Welsh ships, I was hoping to find more images of Newport built ships. . This Smack lying near to a the quay wall in Conwy has a name on her transom. The name **John** can be seen sand the vessel is probably the 39 ton smack of the same name, built Barmouth in 1865. Her dimensions of 57 feet long, 17.6 beam and relatively shallow draft of 6.5 feet. do look like the proportions as seen in the photograph. In 1875 her master was H.Ellis and her owner J.Roberts. Her timbers are in good condition and not as heavy a vessel as the earlier Newport vessels. In fact if you look carefully at the size of the timbers and thickness of the bulwalks you can see that this vessel would not meet the exacting standards that were met by the Newport builders. Photograph © National Library of Wales, probably taken before 1880.

**Maria** .Schooner 64 ton. Built at New Quay 1859 (?). This is somewhat confusing and maybe built 1849. Lloyds 1865 has a 65 ton schooner built at New Quay in 1849 with L. Davies as master and Davies & Co' as owners. Another is in the same Lloyds register 1865, a smack built in Wales in 1795 (probably Pwllheli) a 24 ton Smack D.Rees captain and Davies owner that was broken up in 1885. The fate of the schooner is not known.

**Maria & Martha** Sloop 69 ton. Built at Fishguard 1808. In Lloyds Register 1812 as Sloop 68 tons built at Fishguard four years before . Master Captain W.Evans with owners as Evans and Co. She was classified A1 and traded with Liverpool. In Lloyds 1826 she is seen again but as **Maria Martha** built 1811 at Fishguard. Sloop of 68 ton master W. Evans with Evans & Co' as owners. She was surveyed in Cork and E1 classified. Fate unknown.

**Margaret**. Snow 128 ton. Built at Milford 1830. Lost Baltic Sea 11th July 1836 with men. This was one of the larger of the Newport ships and the fact that she was lost in the Baltic Sea suggests that she was collecting timber for the Newport shipbuilding trade. Timber was the only reason for going to the Baltic. From other ships lost, the route taken was around the north coast of Scotland, avoiding the busy English Channel. In the 1970's I once saw two Norwegian fishing boats in Dunmore East, they had their hulls full of whale meat and were ready to head for home. I asked them which way do they go home and they said always via Scotland.

**Martha.** Brig 123 tons owned Dinas/ Newport. Built Appledore, Devon 1819.

**Mary**. Sloop 26 ton. Built at Aberayron 1778.

**Mary & Eliza**. Sloop 129 ton. Built at Carmarthen 1824. Not seen in Lloyds Ship Register in 1827.

**Mary Ann** Smack 25 ton. Built at Milford 1866. Registered no. 53151   Owned by Captain James of the Ship Inn, Newport she was wrecked at Abermawr, North Pembrokeshire in 1906. In her 50$^{th}$ year the **Mary Ann** was sailing in ballast on her way to Swansea when she hit rocks near Strumble Head. No lives were lost and the coastguard may have helped with saving the two men on board. The vessel was damaged and had lost her rudder but the next day, 14$^{th}$ May 1906, the wrecked smack lifted off the rocks and drifted quietly onto Abermawr beach on a gentle northerly. Other reports suggest that Samuel Griffiths, her master, purposely ran the smack onto Abermawr beach where the smack broke up and the rescue occurred. Whatever the circumstances the wreck was purchased on the beach by Harries of Tregwynt. He wanted the timbers from the vessel to rebuild his Woollen Mill just up the road.    Samuel Griffiths of Newport, who was already 74 years of age, had been captain of the **Mary Ann** for much of her considerable lifetime. He was a true man of the sea and did not wish to give up his lifestyle. A few months later he was captain of **Anne,**   another smack of similar size, bought from North Wales as a replacement. It was not his year as this vessel was also wrecked off Strumble Head in October of the same year. . Captain Griffiths nearly lost his life again in the incident. He owed his life to the Lifeboat crew of the St Dogmael's rowing Lifeboat who picked him from the vessel as it was sinking fast. See details written up under **Anne.**

**Mary and Margaret,** Brig, 131 (125) ton. Built at Kincardine 1807. In 1851 Lloyds Register with D.James as master and Havard Owned.

**Milford.**   Sloop 40 ton. Built St Dogmaels 1788. A vessel of this name was lost in 1801 near Milford Haven. The **Milford,** Captain Richards, foundered on 26 January 1801 when on a voyage from Newport (unspecified) to London with a general cargo and iron. Crew saved.

**Mary and Margaret**   Brig, 131 tons built 1807 Kincardine, Scotland. Memorial 19 at St Mary's Church has a gravestone giving us the following information "William Jones, Newport Master aged 44 died 1847 .02.08 " The dates and Lloyds register tell us that William Jones was master in 1846 and that the ship was lost around the date on the gravestone. Jones and Co of Newport were owners and the vessel was under the Milford registry. The fate of the vessel is not known but she likely was wrecked around the Uk coast on that date in 1847. This vessel probably carried a crew of eight men and if these were from Pembrokeshire, some may have been lost on the same date

**Minerva of Newport.**   Built at Newport or Pembroke 1811. Brigantine 102 ton  In Cardigan Register 1812 no. 2. 1825 no. 82. 1838 no. 7 .Dimensions: 62 feet long.  A new deck was fitted in 1842. Listed in Lloyds Register of 1850 and 1854 as Brig, J.Davies master and Havard owned.  Classified AE1.  During the 1829 to 1834 era we see Havard as a master and trading from Glasgow, Liverpool and Cork. Still in Cardigan Register in 1854.  In Lloyds 1825, 1832 and 1854 she is listed as a Brig being built in Newport in 1811 with Havards still owners and Rowlands as master.  This could have been built in Newport by Havards but my original notes say she was built in Pembroke. This is most odd as Havards were building their own ships of this size in 1811.   There was a Barque **Minerva** lost off Formby in 1839, crew saved, vessel lost.
Another ship of this name was lost near Danzig, Prussia in December 1831. Another **Minerva** was lost foundered on a voyage from Galway to Cork on  9th January 1835. Crew rescued.
Not to be confused with sloop 42 ton **Minerva** built Cardigan 1814 owned by T.Davies, that had T.Evans as master in 1825 In 1836 another T.Davies as master  Also smack **Minerva.** 25 ton built 1797 in Cardigan but then Bideford Registry.

**Oak.** Flat 33 ton. Built Queensferry 1840.  No other information .

**Margaret**   Built in Milford Haven in 1830 and Newport owned. Schooner.  One of the memorial gravestones in St Mary's Church states that the master John Davies (of Newport) aged 31 died in the Baltic. It seems that this was the ship's first major voyage and that it was lost in the Baltic Sea when returning to London on 11th July 1836. "The schooner was driven ashore at "Hornbeck", Denmark. She was on a voyage from Danzig to London. **Margaret** was later refloated and taken in to Helsingør, Denmark.  Fate Unknown. *(The Times (16195). London. 30 August 1836. col C, p4).*

**Mathildis** 133 ton Not built Newport but at New Quay, Cardigan in 1842. I had this listed as a Brig of 133 tons, having Newport owners  The schooner **Mathildis** built and from Newquay in 1845-6 Lloyds Register with master Phillips. 126 ton built 1842. Also seen in Lloyds Register 1856-1858 as master Joshua James 126 ton built at New Quay in 1842 and registered at New Quay with Philipps & Co. as owners. She was last surveyed in Cardigan in 1857 after repairs had been done to her. This is the **Mathildis** lost in the Great Gale of 25-26 October 1859.

**Mathildis** of New Quay painted in Naples and wrongly named **Mathilda.** She had Newport owners when she was lost.

The hurricane is described in the *Pembrokeshire Herald dated 28th October 1859,*" Very few of the oldest inhabitants recollect a more violent storm. FISHGUARD. On Tuesday night this place was visited with an almost unprecedented hurricane. On Tuesday the sea was like a sheet of glass, the weather clear, vessels passing up and down the channel, and Snowdon and other mountains in North Wales quite perceptible, which is always a true sign of wind and rain. The gale commenced about six p.m., and the rain came down in torrents, without inter- mission. till the following morning.

The damage done to the houses is fearful; every house in the town, more or less, has been injured; hundreds of panes of glass are broken the weather fish, on the Town Hall, (this is the weather vane in the shape of a herring) which has stood many a heavy storm for the last twenty- five years was blown away the large slabs under the roof of our church were blown down to the churchyard, oak and other trees uprooted; indeed, the damage done is beyond description.

The shipping in the harbour suffered more or less, and been the cause of shaking the foundation of our beautiful bridge, and the recent new building of this handsome structure is gone to pieces. Lower Fishguard suffered considerably. The road to the new pier was washed away, boats and wreck thrown by the sea to the doors of our inhabitants, and many of the houses half full of water.

The storm did great damage at Goodwick two sloops were blown up near to Goodwick Marsh. The loss of life and property on sea has been frightful. On Wednesday morning a small vessel was seen in the offing making tor this place, which proved to be the **Ellen and Mary,**' of Newquay, and was brought safe to harbour. Three more schooners safely anchored in the road. A smack, the **Abeona** of Cardigan, went against the rocks outside the 'Cow and Calf,' crew saved, three in number. small vessel went down outside of Pencaer, crew perished. The greater part of a large ship from 1,000 to 1,500 tons burthen **(Charles Holmes)**, came in to Abermawr one body was washed a-shore about the same time. A quantity of cloth and blankets has been picked up, and more are to be seen floating A Danish barque ran into Porthgain, went to pieces, and carried off the small pier; crew, thirteen in number, saved. At Cwm yr Eglwys , to the eastward of this place, a schooner and a sloop were lost, all hands perished. Six bodies were washed ashore on Wednesday evening, and more are floating about. The loss of life and property is immense the sea, today, between Dinas Head and Strumble Head is covered with wreck, human bodies, and valuable things from the different vessels lost. Does not all this loss of life and property call on our Government to have this bay surveyed for a Harbour of Refuge between Holyhead and Milford? "

The Cardiff Times 29th October 1859 adds another snippet of information to the Dinas Head shipwrecks. It suggests that three small vessels and the schooner **Mathildis** were all lost.

" The havoc on the Welsh coast proves to have been more destructive to life and property, than has been represented, and it is feared that almost a similar catastrophe to that of the Royal Charter has occurred on the lower portion of St Georges channel off the Pembrokeshire coast. The coasters on this section of the coast suffered severely. Three small vessels were driven ashore near Dinas Head and all hands drowned. The schooner **Mathildis** of Newquay was also lost, with all hands, and the bodies were found amongst the wreck."

One of the wrecks on Dinas Head was the Smack **Swansea Trader** a 36 ton, 31 year old vessel carrying a cargo of roofing slates. She was registered in Swansea, built in Bideford in 1828 and carried a crew of three. Captain Gammon and two others were drowned. Gammon is a notable name in Mumbles, especially with the history of the Mumbles Lifeboat. In 1858 Elizabeth Ace, of Mumbles Lighthouse married a William Gammon, who would undoubtedly be related to the Captain Gammon lost on Dinas Head. However in May 1859 there was another vessel with coal arriving in Swansea named **William** that had a captain Gammon as master.

One of the other small vessels wrecked on Dinas Head in the 1859 gale was the New Quay smack **Ann & Mary.** She also had three crew all drowned, their bodies being recovered by Mr Raymond, who farmed the Island Farm.

Over the next few days bodies washed ashore and one was carried up to the church using a wheelbarrow. A further seven bodies were subsequently washed ashore or recovered from the cliffs. Two burials are recorded in the Dinas Burial register for 30th October – 'Unknown drowned in a shipwreck during a terrific gale October 25th 1859. Abode, both Cardiganish as supposed'.

There are owner details of the **Mathildis** and her dimensions in
*www.peoplescollection.wales/items/45146* , 96 tons burthen.
1 deck, 2 masts, length 70 ft 4 inches: breadth taken above the
main wales (gunwales) 20 ft 5in: depth of hold 10 ft 3 in;
schooner, rigged with a standing bowsprit, square sterned, carvel
built, woman's bust head, official number 13144. The **Mathildis**
when built had all New Quay owners but Newport ownership
may have been added later. She certainly traded with Newport.
She was carrying a cargo of culm when wrecked in 1859.
Six crew members were lost, including the master Joshua Jones,
his stepson, and Owen Davies from Fron-wig, her loss deeply
touched the New Quay community.

This terrific tempest was a revolving storm. Joshua Jones, captain
of the **Mathildis** would have known the coastline well and when
the storm started may have taken shelter off Cym yr Eglwys.
Once the storm moved to NNW force 12, Dinas Head gave no
shelter and the schooner was soon wrecked on the rocks to the
right hand side of Cwm yr Eglwys.

There are two stone built Victorian houses on the right hand side
of the straight road leading down to Cym yr Eglwys. Before they
were renovated in the 1980's at least two of them had ship's
timbers in the roof of their kitchen areas. These houses were built
about 1870 and there is a good chance that these timbers were
salvaged from the **Mathildis.**

**Richard & Mary.** Smack 18 ton. Built at Pembroke Dock. 1848.
On 14th October 1854, this smack was wrecked at Bettws Point
near to the sand bar of Newport. After stranding on the bar in a
North East storm force 10, this smack anchored but then she
parted her chain and was driven onto the Point. She lay half
submerged in the tide for two weeks, her cargo of culm being
destroyed. She was raised in November and taken to the beach,
one assumes at Bettws below where the Lifeboat House is now.
Whether or not she was rebuilt has not been ascertained.
( *Reference. Larn and Larn Wreck Index 2000.)*

**Royal Recovery** Brig 82 ton Built Leith 1789. In 1805 Lloyds there Brig 82 tons that was built in Leith in 1789, Smith and Co owners and traded Liverpool to Venice. The Newport owned Royal Recovery was lost off the Smalls when taking cargo and passengers from Youghal to Cardiff on 22nd April 1832. The Brig developed a leak and sank but all passengers and crew were saved by the **London** a passing ship, going from Liverpool to London, master Genders. ( *Larn and Larn Wreck Index 2000.)*

**Sarah**. Schooner 124 ton. Built Cardigan 1842. In 1865 a schooner **Sarah,** sank in the Bay of Biscay when sailing from Milford to Ireland. All saved including captain Mendus Potter's Electric News 29th November1865. Another **Sarah** with a John Jones master was lost after hitting Chapel Rock Porthkerry Bay,Ireland in 27th December 1873 Crew launched their own boat and got ashore safely. Sarah sank near the rock.

**Shannon Packet** Sloop 37 ton . Built Low Island, Limerick, Ireland in 1827 Into Cardigan registry 1841, owned by Thomas James of Dinas in 1847. The vessel was lost Nash Sands on 20th October 1847 and T.James may have been lost with his vessel.

**Speculator**. Sloop 76 ton. Built Aberystwyth 1804. In Lloyds Register of 1808 this is given as a sloop built in Wales in 1804 of 72 ton with captain/owner as Williams then there is an addition of C.Langdon as master. In 1816 Lloyds master now B.Thomas with owners Capt & Co. . Sloop 72 tons built 1804. Fate unknown.

**Speedwell** Sloop 42 ton. Built Traethmawr, Merionethshire. 1780. But with Newport owners. A **Speedwell** was lost 1810 in Cardigan Bay, Captain Jones and another **Speedwell** of Nevin was wrecked on the West Mouse off Holyhead in October 1854.

**Susannah.** Sloop. 29 ton. Built Carmarthen 1782. On 17th October 1812, this vessel was driven onshore near Milford Haven and she went to pieces. Captain Rees. She was on a voyage from Newport to Cork. Her crew and cargo were saved.

**Swallow** . Sloop 30 ton. Built Barmouth 1783. I do not know if it is the same vessel but a sloop with this name was abandoned by her crew off Milford, when she became dismasted on a voyage from Waterford to Swansea on 3rd June 1809. Captain Crawford. *(Lloyds List No. 4360)*

**Taff of Twenty Two.** Sloop 26 ton Dinas owned. I think this is a truly delightful name to call a small sloop. Obviously she was built on the banks of the Taff in Cardiff in 1822. Not seen in Lloyds in 1834. However she was lost on the Cardigan Bar 29th October 1851.

**Tivy Lass (Teifi Lass).** sloop 33 ton. Built Cardigan 1840. **Tivy Lass** was lost in Swansea Bay in 1st October 1856, while taking iron ore from Neath to Saltney. She drove ashore and sank on the rocks of Mumbles Head . No lives lost .*(Cardiff and Merthyr Guardian 4th Oct 1856)*

**Pheasant**   Built in New Quay in 1837 but owned by Newport merchants. Sloop, 25 tons . Loss maybe Hells Mouth, Lleyn but the date in uncertain, probably after 1868 and before 1883. Details of another **Pheasant** are found in Lloyds Ship Register in the year 1872 and 1874. **Pheasant** (official no. 14244.) Smack built at New Quay in 1829. 27 tons Dimensions: 43 feet long by 14.0 ft beam by 7.5 ft depth. Master and owner T Briddyr. Cardigan Registered. As my records give a loss date of 1864 in Hellsmouth, I still was not convinced I had found the correct vessel.

This is a photograph of the **Alice Williams** a topsail schooner built by Bevans of Llanelly in 1855. She was lost on Skokholm Island in 1928. This is a more modern and sleeker hull than Newport built schooners such as the **Harmony,** but the rig of both would be similar. Note the repair patches on the sails.
(Photograph courtesy of National Maritime Museum)

Then I found two **Pheasant**s both in the Cardigan register recorded in Lloyds 1863 Register.. One was the Smack built in 1829 (above) but J.Thomas master / owner and the other also a Smack built in Newquay but in 1837. Newport owner master was J. Owens. The following year, 1864. Lloyds lists her again this time with her Dimensions of 40.0 feet long, 13 ft beam and 7.0 ft depth. J. Owens is still her master. I had now to look in newspapers to see if her loss in the Lleyn Peninsular is also recorded. On the 24th March 1864 the **Pheasant**, Owens arrived in Porthdinllaen from Liverpool. On 26th May she had loaded and sailed from Porthdinllaen to go to Liverpool, presumably with a slate cargo.

The 1865/1866/1867/1868 Lloyds all list both vessels, inferring that the Cardigan registrar did not know of her being lost before June 1867. It is noted that T.Briddyr master has gone from Cardigan to Milford Registry in 1866. I failed to find a vessel of this name lost in 1864 but as there was another **Pheasant** built in St. Dogmaels in 1876, I wondered if our smack was lost nearer that date. 30 ton 1876 Captain Jones, Lion House, High Street, St. Dogmaels (via Glen Johnson). On the ships of Pwllheli is a 26 ton smack called **Pheasant**, built or acquired in 1865 that was lost by New Brighton 2 January 1887 . This must be the one normally sailed with T. Briddyr captain. There was no
vessel registered in Lloyds named **Pheasant** in 1883 so the Pwllheli smack could not have underwriters from Lloyds.
My original records said Lost Hells Mouth, North Wales in 1864, but I now have my doubts.

**Samson**  Brig, owned or built in Newport. Memorial gravestone number 60 in St Mary's Church states "Thomas Joshua of Newport, Master of the brig SAMSON from Newport . Remembered died 1826, April 17th. Aged 34. However I have a note that says the vessel was not lost until after 1839. Any more information on this vessel would be  appreciated.

As can be seen above although they all have Newport owners, some of the 64 shares in the vessel may be owned by other people in North Pembrokeshire and Cardigan area.

Amongst the shipping records in the Havard Papers in the National Library of Wales are papers, 1833-1879, relating to the Newport schooners **'Harmony'**, **'Claudia'** and **'Adroit'**, and the Milford brig **'Anne'**. These were found in a desk that had been in Danydre, Newport and acquired by NLW in 1989. The desk was at Danydre when captain David Davies died and his body was brought home from Limerick about December 1855. Mary Davies, his widow, was a sister of Levi Havard, the shipbuilder. For anyone researching Newport built ships these papers are invaluable. From these papers and from the Cardigan Shipping Registers to be seen at the Pembrokeshire Record Office in Haverfordwest I have extracted the following information on two vessels built in Newport in 1814.

**Eliza of Cardigan,** built 1814 by John Havard on the banks of the River Nevern. Dimensions: 71.6 feet long, 22.6 feet beam and 11.9 feet depth. She had one deck and was square sterned. Brig rigged on two masts. Tons burthen 147.82/94 tons ( nearly 148 tons). Her Master Frederick Seaborn. Owners were Frederick Seaborn (master and mariner) John Owen, gentleman. David Stephens - sailmaker of Fishguard. Daniel Evans, David James and Owen Harries, all mariners of Newport. Wlm Williams, Rope maker of Fishguard. Dorothy Harries of Henllys, a widow, John Seaborn -mariner. Anne Williams, Mary Lloyd and Sarah Davies, all widows living in Fishguard. David Evans of Cardigan, mariner, and William John of Newport Monmouthshire- a victualler.

The **Eliza** was Registered De Nova 3/1825 (1st January 125) She was lost Mumbles Head on 1st March 1854. At the time of her loss she was recorded as 135 net tons, and still a Brig rig. She had departed from Waterford in ballast (ie without cargo) and had anchored in Swansea Bay. **Eliza,** parted from her anchors and drove ashore at 5pm, due to stress of weather in wind conditions SE force 10. The seven crew were saved in their own boats. The vessel was insured for £200.

The other vessel built at Newport in 1814 was the **Artuous**. She was built by the only other shipbuilder William Lloyd. Of interest is that, within a few inches, the **Artuose** and the **Eliza** had approximately the same dimensions. Also their 64 share ownership included many of the same names .**Artuose** built Newport 1814. Shipbuilder William Lloyd, son of Thomas Lloyd who was shipbuilder in Newport 1770 to 1790. One deck two masts and square sterned, Brig rigged 157 tons old burthen Dimensions: 72 feet long, 22.8 feet beam and 11.7 feet depth. Master John Wade. Owners: John Wade - mariner of Fishguard. David Stephens -sailmaker of Fishguard and Geo Lloyd - gentleman of Fishguard. The Newport owners were the builder Wlm Lloyd - shipwright and Owen Harries -mariner. Other part owners were from other parts of Pembrokeshire and two were from Swansea. Mary Ann Lloyd - widow, William Williams- ropemaker. Ann Williams-widow. James Morgan- mariner, Thos Stephens-mariner, Thos Phillips -sailmaker and David Harries -mariner, all these being from Fishguard. Thos Harries of Cefn Hendre - farmer, James Harries of Dinas- mariner. John Evans of Reynoldston- farmer. Geo Lloyd of Woodstock- gent. David Bowen of Milford. Thos Harries- mariner Swansea and Edward Davies a brewer from Swansea. As we can see from the list of part owners the **Artuose** was predominantly owned by Fishguard folk and the **Eliza** by Newport owners. We see that in lieu of payment for sails made in Fishguard, David Stephens obtained part shares in both vessels. Ropes for both ships were probably made by the ropemaker William Williams. Ropes would be laid out and wound on the road opposite the top of the Slade called Ropewalk today. The **Artuose** sails were made on the upper floor of 3 Main Street, the large building next to Barfive in Main Street Fishguard. Descendants of the **Artuose** owners were the Solicitors, Walter L Williams that occupied the same building in the 1970's. From the rear windows of the sail loft you get a commanding view of ships entering the harbour.

The **Artuose** was newly registered into the Milford register in 1837 (no. 13 in the Customs Book). She is listed in Lloyds Ship Register, (ship no. 1686) in 1874 and 1875 having her captain still as John Wade. Her Dimensions are given as 68.8 x 20.0 x 12.2 feet. John Wade added to his ownership when he acquired the 1/16 share on the death of Mary Ann Lloyd. The ship carried a crew of ten men and was wrecked on Cardiff Flats in 8th March 1876. Searching the newspapers of the day I have failed to find any further details of this sinking, however it is assumed that none of the crew were lost.

This could be the same person as Captain Wade who was the master of the Cardigan vessel **Eclair** from 1843 to 1846. In October 1844 Captain Wade was married at Ferwig to Eliza, the eldest daughter of Thomas Williams, tanner and farmer. In February 1846 the Eclair had a new master. Looking at the ownership of the Artuose in 1821 we see that the owner is W.Wade and the captain is J Wade. It is not clear if this is John Wade or James Wade but it would undoubtedly be father and son. The building of a brig the size of **Artuose** would take about six to eight months. Three large vessels were launched in the year 1814 at Newport, whereas other years we see only one or two. The original Havards' ship yard was on the Sheephill side of Afon Nyfer (River Nevern) .In fact the word Sheephill may be a corruption of Ship Hill. Originally I had always assumed the Havard yard and the Lloyds shipyard were both situated near the present Boat Club. However I now believe them to have been next to each other not far from the limekiln on the far side of the river near the bridge. The Havards did own land and a quay wall near to where the Boat Club is now. This is also where there was a saw pit and storage for coal, known to be in existence around 1880. I now surmise that all the last Havard ships were built on land near to the Parrog Car Park. There was a decline of building the ships at Bryncyn from 1830's.

**Excel of Milford**
This was a large brig of 221 tons built in Newport in 1854. Dimensions 92.5 feet long, 21.6 feet beam and 14.4 feet depth. One deck and had a figurehead of a female to waist height.(Bust). She was built by Levi Havard who had 4/64 th shares. Master was David Nicholas who had 16 of the 64 shares (ie 25% ownership). Other owners were Phoebe Havard of Newport who was then a widow. Mary Roland of Newport also a widow of Newport. David and Thomas David of Cardigan. David Davies and David Griffiths of Newport. The last owner recorded was a shipping agent of Liverpool. Levi Havard was an executor of William Havard, late of Newport deceased.

The ship is in Lloyds Register of 1865-1866 as a Brig with D. Nichols as master, 222 ton with same dimensions but says built 1853 Milford. The entry has a line through Milford, her owners as Nicholas and her classification suggesting that she was lost late in 1865. She was last surveyed in Liverpool with a voyage intended to the West Indies. Her port registration still as Milford. The only other reference that might be the same vessel is in New York ship news ... Brig **Excel,** (Br.,) Nicolas, Algoa Bay, South Africa 64 days out. with wool to order. Marine Intelligence New York 4th Dec 1863. Her Fate is unknown.

The second largest vessel built at Newport was the Schooner **Hope** in 1827, she was 182 tons. Despite the size all the ships built in Newport had one deck. That was the construction they were used to building so that is what they continued to build. The lofting dimensions seen in the Havard Papers relate to just two sizes of vessels. It would seem that both shipbuilding yards in Newport stuck to the same design.

*Photo ©
Huw Evan*s

A 1/4 " foot of copy of the **Ontario** built on Llanddewi Aberarth beach in 1831. A 53 ton Smack, 48'10"Length, 17'2", beam and depth of hold 8'3" Huw Evans constructed this superb impression. The Smacks and Sloops built by the Havards were a few feet smaller but would have looked very similar. Straight stemmed and Square transom, bulbous and beamy hull to take the ground. Tanned coloured sails on a Gaff Rig. This is the simplest of rigs and was usually sailed by a master (owner) a mate and a boy. The boy was usually a nephew or from the same family as the men and aged 14-20 he would have been doing his 'apprenticeship' for becoming a mariner.

Donald Davies wrote about Cardigan vessels for the local County Echo newspaper in the 1970's. I met him a few times to talk about historical maritime matters. I failed to ask him where he collected all his detailed information from. Amongst his writings he mentions the Cardigan brigs **Hope** of 129 tons and **Eliza,** 146 tons, master William Davies, both being captured by French privateers.

It was the year 1814 when **Eliza** was built in Newport. This is the same year as the **Eliza** was bought back from internment by the French. Thomas Davies had to pay for 21 months of food and lodging to the French before he could see Captain William Davies and the crew of the **Eliza** again.

When looking through the Ship News in the newspapers of old, it is interesting to see which ports the ships visited, especially if their cargos are recorded as well. After the ships name the masters name is given. This is like an added identification, as so many of the sloops had the same name. The only way the traders and owners could track their goods on a voyage was to follow the progress by reading the shipping news in the newspapers. The news gave the ship's progress around the coast, when the ship entered and departed from each port. But newspapers were expensive, costing three or four day's wages. Consequently Reading Rooms and libraries were set up so that the daily and weekly news could be followed by those interested. I would guess the Memorial Hall was used as the Reading Room in Newport.

A typical entry under Shipping News would be as such . 18th March 1837, departing from Neath was the **Hopewell,** Lewis, from Cardigan on her way to Cardiff with oats. **Friendship,** Stevens and **David**, Lewis, cleared out for Cardigan.

One such Reading Room is still to be seen on the seafront road in Barmouth. In a traditional tin shed the Sailors Institute still operates a reading room and a billiard table in a similar way to how it was done a century ago. By joining such a cooperative the cost of reading the most up to date news on the ships travelling and trading around the coast could be minimised.

This is a painting of **Agenoria**. (© Ceredigion County Museum) Built at Newport in 1834. She was 117 ton Schooner and had the typical hull dimensions of many of the ships built at Newport,

It shows a two masted vessel with both masts carrying fore and aft sails, hence a Schooner rig. The foremast also has two square rigged topsails. These are carried on very wide yard arms, typical on a Brig rig before 1840. Indeed many of the Newport ships were Brig or Brigantine rigged but these would always need a few more men to handle sails than the simpler schooner rig. Later topsail schooners would carry much smaller square rigged sails aloft. There is a bowsprit and a jib-boom to carry fore sails. Note that the second or main mast that carries the largest sail is raked back at a slightly greater angle than the foremast. All Newport vessels had just one deck and helmed in the open using a large tiller. She would be sailed by 7 men In 1854 her rig was changed to that of a Brigantine which meant removal of the fore and aft sail on the foremast and replaced with yard arms and more square sails on this mast. She traded around the Irish sea and Bristol Channel ports and was lost in 1880. Her age when lost was 46 years old which was not unusual for such well-built and well managed vessels.

In 1841, the Havards made up and costed the specifications of a 340 ton paddle steamer. The specifications were produced but the vessel was never built by them. From the Havard Papers at the NLW I made some notes about the timber specifications The steamship was to be 150 feet long with 20 feet beam and 11 foot depth. Her keel was to be made up of three lengths of American elm and two lengths of English elm. The Paddle beam was a 15 inch square beam made of Silesian oak. This same oak for the floor and foot holds. The Transom and framing timber to be constructed of English Oak, that had to be sound and free from blemish. Treenails (Trunnels) of Danzig Fir. It was well known that you do not use iron nails in oak timber, but I did not know that Danzig pine wood was the most appropriate timber for the wood trunnels. Silesian Oak was the special timbers of Pedunculate oak trees *(Quercus robur)* in Poland and obviously had to be imported from the Baltic together with the Danzig fir *(Pinus sylvestris)*. The English oak (*Quercus robur*) could be found in the local estates although finding good oak timber anywhere in the UK from 1660's onwards was a problem as it had already been used up in the shipbuilding industry.

The Bowen estates, especially Llwyngwair were carefully planted with trees to be managed for future generations. Hazel *(Corylus avellana)* was planted in Cockshut woods. Hazel was coppiced for wattle or withy fencing, to provide kindling and nuts. As the name of these woods implies the woods provide cover for woodcock. A line of large sweet chestnuts *(Castanea sativa)* can be seen on one hill. Apart from the medicinal properties of chestnuts the timber was used for making fence posts as the tannin is a natural preservative and stakes do not rot in the ground. Many of the Newport seamen would, during the winter months, be employed cutting and collecting timber to keep the fires burning in Llwyngwair Manor. They would be aware of the importance of keeping an eye out for frame timbers for the ships being built on the estuary. Timber was both an export and an import cargo for the trading vessels of Newport. I guess surplus timber coming from the Baltic could have been sawn at Newport and then sent for house building in Ireland.

Although the details for building the steamship to be built in 1841 by the Havards stated Danzig fir, this is not what Lloyds of London were specifying for sailing ships in 1838. Lloyds Register specified that all treenails are to be made of good English or African oak, of locust or other hard wood, but in no case is Baltic or American oak or elm to be used. They also gave specifications on fastenings placements and the thickness of hull planks for different sized vessels. I have failed to find out who the Havards were commissioned by, to produce a quotation price for a steamer. They may have done the exercise for themselves as no other person is mentioned in the documents. If so it is a great shame that it was not pursued as not many yards were building steamships in 1841. Bristol and Glasgow had already started building the first steamships, more than a decade before. Nevertheless it could have completely changed Newport's direction had the Havards started building steamers in 1841. Newport ship builders were used to building in wood and many of the paddle steamers being built by 1841 were starting to be built with all iron hulls. The Havards could see this change and thought that they just could not compete with the established industrial ship builders. Twenty years went by before the newly formed Aberayron Steam Navigation Co were to get their first steamer, **Prince Cadwgan** built in Glasgow, wood clinker on iron frames. This made the Cardigan merchants sit up and a few years later in 1869 they too had their first steamer, the all iron built vessel ss **Tivyside.** Thus started a new chapter for West Wales maritime trade. Iron (not steel) built sailing ships and steamers were being constructed at the larger industrial ports in Scotland and Humberside. Building ships out of wood was starting to decline. There was, however, one notable exception. Portmadog, continued building schooners out of wood and produced a new and different breed of fast wooden sailing ship that had never been seen before around the Welsh coast.

This is a painting of a Snow but is similar to what the Brig **Anne** 161 tons, would have looked like. The Brig **Anne** had dimensions of Length of Keel 72.6 Feet, Breadth moulded of 22.6 feet. Depth of Hold 12.4 feet. Height in the middle of the Hold 13.6 feet. Height of Transom 13.0 feet, Length of Transom (I assume breadth) 17.0 feet. The extreme length of the foremast 51 feet. 31.6 feet from deck to Truss. 12.0 inside the hold. Head "D" 7.6 feet. The main mast extreme length was 52.6 feet with 11.6 in the hold and a Head of 7.6 feet. Top Masts to the shoulder 24.6 plus a head "D" of 4.3 feet. Top Gallant Masts to the shoulder 14.0 feet Royal Masts and Heads 13.0 feet. Gib- boom from cap to shoulder 16 feet, from shoulder to shoulder 9.0 feet Extreme Length Bowsprit 38 feet. Boom length 38.6 feet, Gaff length 28.6 feet. Fore yard 48.0 feet, Top sail yards 33.0 feet. Top Gallant yards 23.0 feet, Royal Yards 18.0 feet.

Before survey **Anne** had a carpenters measurement of 220 tons. Her old measurement was 181 tons and a new measurement of 161 tons. When she was launched and ready for sea, that meant complete with a frying pan from Havard's shop her cost was £13-15-3½ per ton in old measurement. She cost to build £1629-0-0 using a calculation of 181 tons @ £9 per ton . We can see from the Accounts for the building of the Schooner **Agenoria** that the actual costs also worked out at £9 per ton.

This is an early photograph by Henry Fox Talbot. It shows the stern view of a Brig, dried out on the sand probably outside Swansea in 1844. This is very similar to the size of Brig built at Newport and clearly shows how the hull was designed for taking the ground between tides. I think there is a 10% chance that one of these two vessels could be a Newport ship. The nearer vessel is a similar tonnage schooner which has dried out in a more upright
Position.

Photograph by Henry Fox Talbot 1844 National Museum of Wales, probably in Swansea Harbour.

## Building Account in 1846 of the Schooner Adroit.

| £ s d | |
|---|---|
| 941 10 2 | Levi Havard shipbuilders bill |
| 99 12 3 | Smith's Bill for chains and anchors |
| 63 19 0 | Ropemaker's Bill |
| 87 0 0 | Sailmakers Bill |
| 27 12 8 | Blockmaker's Bill |
| 52 25 8 | John David's Smiths Bill |
| 33 9 7 | Mr Levi Vaughan's Bill |
| 10 10 8 | Mr John Acraman's Bill |
| 11 13 0 | Lloyd & Davies, Cardigan |
| 5 01 1 | Mr James Evan's of Cardigan |
| 5 13 6 | Mr Levi Havard's Shops |
| 01 7 | Mr James Griffiths |
| 2 13 4 | Cooper's Bill £1 Staves £1-13-4 |
| 1 15 8 | Painters Bill Table £1 Boards 15/8 |
| 15 11 | Deal & Lining for Cabin |
| 1 07 11 | John Davies shop (incl skylight 7.0 shillings) |
| 14 0 | Expense getting Masts and Spars from Fishguard |
| 10 9 | James Thomas for carriage of goods 5/- Leather 5/9 |
| 1 02 0 | Men for Scraping the Vessel 10/- Tarpauling 12/- |
| 9 0 | Sand 6/4 Tarbrush 1/3 Black Paint 1/3 |
| 7 8 | Earthenware 6/6 Twin and Brooms 1 s 3 p |
| 8 5 0 | Riggers Bill |
| 10 11 | David Parry Smith's Bill (Ship's Bell? ) |
| 3 9 8 | Boy Attendance |
| 2 10 0 | Livery Allowance |
| 1 10 0 | Capt David James for Survey |
| 2 17 6 | Ballasting the Vessel |
| 2 8 6 | Customs Cardigan |
| 8 0 0 | Bread and Butter |
| 16 0 0 | Master Attendance. |

**£ 1400 12 9** Grand Total for this ship surveyed at 157 tons

This is about £9 per ton If Havard was giving an estimate of building cost to a client this is what he would quote .£9 per ton.

## Some factors learnt from researching these Newport vessels.

As nearly all the Newport built vessels came under the Registration port of Cardigan, many of them have been categorized (by previous authors) as Cardigan built.

The two shipyards in Newport built a total of at least 80 vessels.

The majority of vessels built came into two categories; either a Sloop of 35 to 39 tons or a two masted ship of 90 to 120 tons. They were all carvel construction. All were pure sailing ships. No steamships were built at Newport. It was not unusual for trading schooners to add a donkey engine to aid with loading and unloading of cargo and to help with getting the anchor up. However I have come across no Newport built ships that had such refinements. Nor have I found any that had auxiliary engines fitted in their latter life.

All the ships built had a draught of 13 feet or less, ensuring that they could pass over both Cardigan and Newport sand bars at high water.

They were very well built and were strong and sturdy vessels, many of them lasting more than 45 years old before they were lost.

The majority of the vessels would be owned by a consortium of owners, that all knew each other. The master of the vessel would often have the biggest share of the ownership.

Many of them traded between Bristol, Liverpool and the Irish ports. Occasionally the bigger vessels would sail to the Mediterranean and others to the Baltic ports. I get the impression that if a long or new voyage was undertaken, that the Newport boats would go in tandem, ie two vessels buddy sailing. This would make sense as someone would know the route and know which people to trade with. Having ships the same size ensures that the crew are familiar with sailing them and they are going to sail at similar speeds.

# TOWN OF CARDIGAN.

## To be Sold
### BY AUCTION,

On Monday, March 2nd, 1840,

THE

# WRECK

OF THE

## BRIG, PERSEVERANCE,

OF SOUTHWOLD,

(JOHN MAGUL, Master)

Also, Sails, Rigging, Anchors, Chains, and Cordage, one Boat, Mast, Yards, &c., &c.

N.B. For particulars apply to Mr. D. Davies, Lloyd's Agent, Cardigan.

ISAAC THOMAS PRINTER, ST. MARY STREET, CARDIGAN.

Discovered in Isaac Thomas printers shop, when it was being sold in the 1960's.

**Voyages undertaken by *Exley* 29 ton Sloop in 1870. .**

To get an idea of the kind of voyages the Sloops were doing I have picked one 29 ton sloop 47 feet long and looked at her voyages made in 1870. This sloop was not built in Newport but acquired by Eliza Berriman of West Street, Newport in June 1861. Built in Hull the vessel was already ten years old and was now registered in Cardigan (6/1861) The vessel was sailed by just three, the master John Jones aged 57, the mate, David Llewellyn aged 59 and a boy of 14 named John Thomas. The master and mate were both from Newport, I am not sure if the boy was also. What we do know that this was John Thomas's first ship. It was his apprenticeship to learn the ropes, how to navigate the coast, how to understand the weather and the tides.

In 1870 March 20th They sailed from Newport to Milford Haven and back and hence to Llanelly. April 1st sailed from Llanelly to Newport and hence to Pembrey. April 10th sailed from Pembrey back to Newport. April 15th Newport to Milford Haven and back. April 24th, Newport to Milford Haven and back hence to Llanelly May 5th from Llanelly to Newport and back to Llanelly.
May 10th sailed from Llanelly to Newport hence to Milford and back to Newport sailed hence to Llanelly and thence to Newport. June 25th from Newport to Llanelly and back   June 30th from Newport to Llanelly and back. July 1st again another trip to Llanelly. July 16th Llanelly to Newport to Milford . July 30th Milford to Newport to Llanelly, August 11th Llanelly to Newport to Milford  August 19th Milford to Newport to Llanelly September 16th Llanelly to Newport to Milford September 26th Milford to Newport and back. October 7th Milford to Newport. Two days later the men finished for the year on 10th October. The men were paid off and had to find alternative employment in the winter months until 20th March when they would start sailing the **Exley** again for the 1871 season.  That is 18 trips that summer, an astonishing mileage.

It is unfortunate that I have not got records of the cargo the **Exley** carried on these trips. The voyages are pretty routine going from Newport to either Milford or Llanelly and back again. I have sailed from Fishguard to Milford and back many times. I have also sailed Milford to Tenby and Milford to Swansea, in a small yacht that would sail at speeds equivalent to a 29 ton sloop. What I find fascinating is that every week during the summer of 1870, the **Exley** was sailing around the Pembrokeshire coast. It was in the Spring of the following year that she was lost. My only details are **Exley** of Newport 29 tons lost Pencaer 3rd April 1871.

A coastline that is one of the hardest to sail anywhere in the UK. It necessitates traversing both Ramsey and Jack Sounds, particularly hazardous places for the unwitting.
The journey is like travelling around three sides of a square. Whatever the wind direction, you will be having it on the beam, behind you, or you are fighting into it. These heavy buff bowed transport ships were not good at sailing and a maximum speed of 6 knots was exhilarating. It is impossible to sail around Pembrokeshire with the tide against you. Thus for half the time you need to anchor to wait a tide.
More than a handful of Newport and Cardigan smacks have been lost in Ramsey Sound. Not only did the local coasting trading sloops use Ramsey Sound as the convenient short cut around St David's but it was also an important sheltering spot and a place to collect fresh water. Locally it was called the Island Roads and to others as the Waterings. Ivor Arnold, who farmed Ramsey around 1908 noted that following some rough weather when vessels were stormbound in Goldtop (sometimes referred to as Goultrop) or Milford Haven he counted no less than 200 sailing vessels coming up through Ramsey on one tide. Today Ramsey Sound may not see 30 sailing vessels passing through in a whole year. This shows the density of small trading vessels around Pembrokeshire in the early part of the Twentieth Century.

One of the reasons I learnt some Welsh was to converse with the older folk to learn more about the maritime history of North Pembrokeshire. I met up with a ninety year old builder in the 1980's who explained to me something about the unloading process using horse and cart. If timber was being unloaded then a long wagon was needed. An additional horse was needed to slowly walk the unladen wagon through the deep water to be alongside the vessel as the tide ebbed. In Fishguard and that means Lower Fishguard, the Brodog Timber Co. had one specific large horse they would use to lead the other horses into the water. Additionally the horses would be trained to move forwards or backwards on command from the ship's bell. I wish I had paid more attention to what he told me, then I would have learnt what two rings on the bell meant! When the cart was full the bell would be rung so many times to tell the horse it was time to take the load to the timberworks at the bottom of the Slade. So important was the training of horses to pull carts in and out of the seawater that it was incorporated into the local regattas. A great assortment of fun, games and contests were included in both Dinas and Newport regattas. Dinas regatta had one event where there was a prize to the person who could lead a donkey into the deepest water!

The Great Famine in Ireland between 1845 and 1852. Caused by the reliance of the poor on potatoes which were decimated with blight. One million Irish poor died and another 1 million migrated to evade the famine. However it is now recorded that more butter was exported from Ireland during the Famine years than at any other time. It was not the general shortage of food in Ireland that caused 25% of her population to emigrate but the fact that the poor could not afford to buy it. Fifty years later and the arrival of the railway to Fishguard, changed the nature of maritime trade around the coast. Goods then tended to be transported by train, and not by sea. General household goods could now get from Paddington, London to Newport in less than two days.

The Havard family had the main monopoly on trading goods in the town. Since Levi Havard moved to Newport from Milford around 1760 the family have always run the biggest ironmongery store in town. This acted as a ship's chandler, supplying cord, anchors, tar and hardware to the ships. The Havards imported the coal and delivered it to the hearths of the
wealthy in the town. When a ship was built, launched and sold, it had to be complete and ready for sea. Not only was it fully rigged with sails from the Fishguard sailmaker already bent onto the yards but the galley had to have a frying pan as well. All arranged by the Havards. The Havard family have been eminent in medicine. In a list of 1830 traders and merchants, David Havard, druggist, and stamp distributor and Levi Havard - shopkeeper and shipwright are mentioned.

Today the only boats sold by the Havards are kayaks and colourful blow up plastic boats seen hanging up outside their shop in East Street. The family stopped building ships in Newport around the 1850's .Nowadays the descendents not only maintain a hardware and camping shop in the town but also have stables in Dinas where visitors can commence a riding trek up Carningli mountain.

When I was living in Newport in the 1980's I got to know Essex Havard, Well, anyone living there would be familiar with his idiosyncrasies. An unassuming man but certainly a character and a half, and many stories may be told of him. He was both a Town Councillor and a County Councillor. I happened to see him the day the postman had delivered a letter to his house. He asked me if it was a joke and if I knew anything about it, half accusing me of its origin. I looked at the letter and studied the printing on the envelope and said it was no joke. It was definitely an invitation from the Queen for Essex to attend Buckingham Palace! He was being awarded for his outstanding services to Surf Lifesaving. He was a father figure of the Newport Surf Lifesaving Club and had completed (like me) the professional Surf Lifesaving exam to become Britain's oldest fully qualified beach lifeguard. Being over 40 at the time, I struggled with the arduous sea swim and the physicality of the tough exam but Essex had no problems and he was more than twenty five years older than me!

**Lifeboat House.**

Constructed as a direct result of not being able to respond to the stricken crew of the **Oline.** St Dogmaels had a lifeboat and Fishguard had two rowing lifeboats; the Newport people wanted one of their very own. As Brian John states, it was something of a white elephant. Nevertheless it did prove useful on a few sparse occasions.

One of the few active calls made by the Newport Lifeboat is recorded in the *Cambrian News 11th October 1899.* "A violent storm from the south west raged at Cardigan and the neighbourhood on Monday morning last. About 9.30 or 10 p.m. a vessel in distress was sighted off Newport Head, about a mile and a half from a stone called Caregydrewy. The Coxswain of the lifeboat named the **Clevedon,** stationed at Newport, was immediately summoned, but as he lives some distance off on the mountain side, he did not arrive until an hour after. On arriving at the lifeboat house it was found that there was not sufficient water to take the boat out, and so she lay on the river side until three or four a.m, when with great difficulty she was got over the bar. When half way out they exhibited a green light and in a short time were successful in hitching to their mast a rope from the distressed vessel, which proved to be the schooner **Reliance,** of Wexford, dismasted and in ballast, bound for the latter place. The lifeboat was pulled alongside and the crew, consisting of three men, were saved. It was ascertained that one of the crew had been drowned, he having jumped at a life buoy which had been thrown them from a passing barque on the day previous. As the wind and tide was so strong the lifeboat with the rescued occupants and crew made for Cemaes point and lauded at the Ferry Inn, St. Dogmell's, Cardigan, on Tuesday morning. One of the volunteering crew of the lifeboat consisted of Mr J. E. Williams, of Parrog House, Newport, son of Mr P. M. G. Williams, surgeon, and eighteen years of age."

Will Morris was interviewed by the school children in the 1970' and he could relate to the day's when his father was a member of the Lifeboat crew, " As a boy, he was the youngest in the crew. The rowing Lifeboat was very difficult to get out" It was only going to be of use when going to help vessel on a lee shore. Hence as soon as they are afloat they are into a teeth of the wind and waves. To help this situation Will Morris explained. "There was an anchor in the bay, and a rope onto that, and a man on the front of the lifeboat." His job was to haul on the rope to aid the lifeboat to get to seaward. "Sometimes the rope used to break" he added. He remembered the wreck of the **Desdemona** and mentioned that the rocket brigade had to haul the Breeches Buoy cart by horse all the way round by road to reach the other side of the bay. "The **Desdemona** was wrecked on the Blackmares, in 1906. Luckily no lives were lost, but I do remember a young boy who was rescued. My father had him to stay for the night in Manchester House. I was very small but I do remember this boy had fleas. He was a lovely little fellow, but, you see, the conditions on the ship were such that they just couldn't help having these fleas!

"The schoolchildren heard stories about the work women did. "Women went salmon fishing with the seine fishermen, about five women in each boat with about seven men. It was very hard work. It was not a woman's job to drag the nets in, as they were very heavy." When spring cleaning time came, the women would take the carpets over to the stream at Cwm. Spreading them out they could scrub them clean with running water over them all the time. "It was quite an effective Job". The carpets were then left on the slipway to drain and dry.

A curious entry is seen in the County Echo dated 17 March 1910. *The little smack "Waterlily" which has been laid up at Parrog since before Christmas, sailed for a destination which did not transpire.* Is the reporter hinting that the **Waterlily** left Newport with the intention of it being sunk before it arrived at its destination or did it just disappear without trace?

**Shipwrecks.**

There have been scores of vessels wrecked outside the ports of Fishguard and Cardigan, but few near to Newport itself. Oddly, there have been a few vessels that have parted their anchors on the Irish coast and driven across the Channel in a strong Westerly to land unattended on the rocks between Newport and Ceibw. The first recorded wreck at Newport was a Liverpool ship taking a cargo of African ivory to Liverpool. She is documented in Larn's Database as wrecked in Cardigan Bay but the historian Fenton says it was actually at Newport. The ship was the **Venerable** lost on 18th January 1819. The crew and part of the cargo were saved. What is not mentioned is that the crew or some of the cargo were probably slaves. The Liverpool economy at this time was being built up on the Slave Trade. If slaves made up a cargo going to Liverpool, Bristol or London it was never mentioned in the newspapers as it was a taboo subject. Politicians were embarrassed at the wealth it was creating. The Anti-Slavery legislation was to be enforced about 13 years after this shipwreck. There have been a few notable wrecks at Newport. One was the **Desdemona** a schooner carrying 156 tons of clay. She was deliberately run onto Big Beach at Cessigduon in February 1906 after being disabled in two days of storm
Translated and sometimes called The Black Mares is the black patch of mud and stones on the beach opposite Traethmawr beach access point. I have often thought this patch of hard mud could be the remnants of the **Desdemona** cargo. This schooner 79.3 feet long, 20.8 feet beam and 10.2 feet draught knew Newport well, she regularly brought china clay into the port. She was built in Aberystwyth in 1874 (32 years earlier). . There was no loss of life and the cargo was discharged. Everyone considered as she was so badly damaged by being pounded on the beach that she was not worth salvaging and would become a total loss. A photograph of her on the sands is seen at the end of this book.

At the other estuary-end of the beach, to be seen at very low tides are scores of fire bricks. The name GLENBOIG is seen on them, a place near Glasgow. These are obviously bricks jettisoned to make a vessel lighter when it got stuck on the sand bar. They could be bricks from the schooner **Desdemona,** or the ketch **Newland,** or a much smaller sloop delivering fire bricks for the new hearths being built in the Newport houses.

A tragic wreck occurred in 1882 when a schooner from Copenhagen was lost with all her crew on Cat Rock. In tempestuous weather signals of distress were seen when the schooner, already disabled, was trying desperately to keep off the land. St Domaels men responded but a mix up occurred when the Coxswain arrived at the Cardigan Lifeboat station at Ceibach. He had erroneously been informed that his crew were already at the Lifeboat Station waiting to launch. They were not. Some were there but not his full regular crew. Volunteers offered to make up the oarsmen but the Coxswain made the decision to not launch as the conditions were far too dangerous. No help was offered and the schooner was driven towards Dinas Head. When the Fishguard folk heard about the schooner they immediately responded. They had two rowing Lifeboats and picked their older, more easily rowed, lifeboat for the task. They headed out into the teeth of the gale and it took three hours to get round Dinas Head. Unfortunately they arrived too late to be of any assistance. The schooner was driven ashore onto Cat Rock where the Newport Rescue Team were waiting with rocket lines to save the crew. One line did reach the wreck but the **Oline** crew were unable to fix it because of the huge waves pounding across the deck. Then the wreck broke apart and one mast toppled, sending the crew to their deaths in the surf. All five men including Captain Holm were lost.

The incident greatly affected the neighbourhood. The Cardigan folk criticised the St Dogmael's Coxswain for not launching. The RNLI fired the Second Coxswain for not complying with Lifeboat procedures. Retired sea captains, in Cardigan, of which their were many, sent a letter to the newspaper endorsing and supporting the decision of the Coxswain not to launch. They well knew the Lifeboat and the St Dogmael's crew may not have survived the atrocious conditions.

The **Oline** nameboard was found tucked away in Essex's garden shed in 1982. The picture below is of the Newport Cliff Rescue Apparatus Cart. Unfortunately the Board of Trade Brigade failed to rescue the **Oline** crew in 1882.*(Photos Tom Bennett collection)*

**The Board of Trade Rocket Apparatus Cart .**

The first garage stone building next to the slipway at Parrog was built especially for this Rocket Apparatus. This photograph, probably taken about 1899 is at the top of the Parrog slipway next to its stone built shed. The Brigade used to practice four times a year, firing a line across the river and sometimes securing a Breeches Buoy to the pole in the river opposite the Boat Club.

The **Oline,** attempted rescue was a massive undertaking for both Fishguard Lifeboats and their crews. They nearly lost two lifeboatmen in the surf of Newport Bay and broke and lost their steering oar and three other oars. I consider it to be one of the most heroic service launches of the Fishguard Station and yet it does not get a mention on their RNLI service plaque as no lives were saved. Those who watched the **Oline** crew perish vowed that the Newport town would have its own Lifeboat Station, so that such a thing would not happen again. Within two years the Lifeboat Station at Cwm, Newport was built. A Royal National Lifeboat Institution Lifeboat **'Clevedon'** was stationed there for eleven years but performed few rescues. The building was abandoned in 1895, due partly to the difficulty of launching the lifeboat at certain tides. There is only a decent depth of water at the bottom of the slipway for about 8 hours in every 24 hours. The building is now a private residence.

This charming photograph is taken on Newport Regatta Day about 1907. It shows a scene at Cwm as the tide is coming in. All are dressed in their Sunday Best and the boats are preparing for the 'Ladies Rowing Race'; it would be nice to think it was 4 Ladies and a Cox, but the boat on the right looks like it is a Cox and Three Ladies.

**Newport and its Rowing Tradition.**
Newport Regatta probably commenced about 1850. It was one of the main festivities of the year and coincided with the holiday time for the South Wales mining towns and the whole place would be full of tourists. The event always happened at Cwm beach allowing spectators to view the action from an elevated position close the harbour mouth. It was a big annual event and from 1910 the regatta would be organised by the Morris family and then by the Morris Brothers. At other times the brothers would have half a dozen small rowing boats which they would hire out to the visitors. Amongst the activities on Regatta Day were swimming races, diving for plates, an underwater swim race, rowing races for the Ladies, and sailing races. The local people had an advantage because they knew the tides and currents. Some events were solely for local people. In 1972 I was looking forward to the race. The event was always done at full high water. The idea was to dive off the steps at Cwm and see how far upstream you could swim underwater before surfacing. I was all prepared and knew I would do well with at least a 45 meter underwater swim, even with no tide assistance. I think they cancelled the event that year because they had been told a visitor (me) running the local Sub Aqua Club was likely to win the prize! However members of our Sub Aqua Club did do well by training and preparing for the "4 men plus Cox" Down River Rowing Race. For Newport folk it was more important than any Oxford and Cambridge Varsity Race. The course was from the Iron Bridge to Cwm at exactly High Water. The Sub Aqua Club boys with me as Cox trained hard and practiced for three weeks before the event. I remember searching the whole of Pembrokeshire for the 12 foot oars needed, and eventually borrowed a set from Saundersfoot Sea Cadets. The local lads using **"Danny Boy"** were not prepared for the event and were easily beaten. I often think that their humiliation that day made the Newport 'Cwch Hir' team super competitive as they did not allow anyone to beat them in rowing races until the Griffiths brothers retired.

Robin Pratt who was responsible for putting red deer on Ramsey relocated to Esgyn Farm near Llanychaer about 1977. I was visiting Esgyn one day and there were two lads from Porthgain constructing a fibreglass copy of a curragh. This traditional Irish lightweight boat had been found washed up on the west side of Ramsey. Rather intrigued I asked them what they were up to. They said they were building a GRP mould for a 'four man and a cox' sea rowing boat out of it. Tom Sutton and Des Harries had the vision of building a few and racing them at the sea regattas. I immediately applauded the concept but considered the design they were dealing with could be improved upon. Nevertheless they persevered and with sponsorship from Paul Raggett at Solva and encouragement from Newport, Fishguard and St David's the Pembrokeshire Long Boat Regattas started. The whole movement was an immediate success. I was keen for the teams to get Sponsorship and professional advice on how to row and train. I contacted the Welsh Rowing Association coaches and they travelled down to Whitesands to observe the inaugural Round Ramsey Race. They were Olympic coaches based at the Public schools on the Wye and were amazed at the enthusiasm. They gave me a subsequent written report informing me that Sports Council involvement was not possible at that time because the teams were already competing for money prizes and so their amateur status had already been compromised. Their report also mentioned that rowing with a cox is one of the few sports that disabled people can compete on an equal basis with able bodied. They were critical of the type of start adopted at Whitesands where from a rocket start from the Lifeboat the crews ran down the beach to launch their craft into the surf. A disabled Cox would be disadvantaged with that type of running start to a rowing race and that was to be discouraged in future events. By 1990 the Olympic Committee allowed professionals to compete in rowing races. That also changed the funding attitude of the Sports Council for Wales who could now help this new up and coming sport of sea rowing.

When I saw the mould for the first Pembrokeshire Longboat being made, I did not like the shape of the bow or the midship freeboard. I thought a simulated clinker design near the bows to help the boat rise on to a swell or to prevent a bow-wave wetting the freeboard would be preferable. To me there was no shape to the bow to help it cut through the water. Des Harries explained it was from an Irish Curragh that had washed up on the west side of Ramsey Island. He was convinced it was the correct shape, after all the Irish had used them in the Celtic Sea for centuries. His notion was correct and the Celtic Longboat has proved to be a good seaboat, a dry boat even in cross seas and breaking waves. The freeboard is not excessive for the conditions they row them in. Paul Raggett, who was a great supporter of the Longboats in its pioneer days, if alive today, would be well satisfied with the success and development of Longboat racing around the Welsh coast.

**Cwch Hir or Celtic Longboat on the Dinas Head Challenge in 2012.** Newport is in the background. The rowers are keeping a careful eye on the cross sea but the deep freeboard design can easily cope with it. Seas around Dinas Head always demand respect. In an October gale in a yacht I was forced to motor one mile hard out to sea in order to round the headland in safety. Otherwise I would have been beam-on to the waves as in this photograph.

The Newport Rowing lads asked me would I join their management team. I was truly honoured to be invited but told them I was already committed to running a Sub Aqua Club, a Life Saving Club, a Swimming Club, and being the Sailing Secretary at Fishguard Bay Yacht Club. I, together with Huw Evans of Goodwick did, however, organize the first Longboat Rowing Race at Goodwick. Most of the Longboat races were over long courses taking at least an hour of rowing to complete. It was decided to do a short course at Fishguard giving the spectators a better view and an opportunity for the crews to compete over half the usual distance. I thought it was a brilliant idea, to get coxswains into a different rhythm and to get them more experienced at rounding buoys competitively. The more experienced competitors, were less happy as they saw it favoured the more rookie type crew! From day one with the Longboat races, I was explaining that the boats had to conform to a standard and there had to be a lot of rules and regulations to make competition fair. I had experienced all this with Royal Yachting Association Racing Rules, different Class Rules for sailing dinghies, Protest Committees and how to measure craft. In one International Moth Regatta, at Fishguard, one competitor was told to sandpaper the bow of his boat before the race. It had two extra coats of paint on it, exceeding the length of the Class Rules by 1.5 mm. Oddly in that Class the beam can be any length but the overall length bow to transom was critical for the Class Rules and required enforcement by Fishguard Bay Yacht Club.

During the first two years the Longboat competitors said they wanted no Rules and Regulations and did not even want an organizing Committee. I really wanted to get involved but was torn between disassociating myself or helping in the best way I was able. The first really big event was the Round Ramsey Race. It started with the St David's Lifeboat firing a rocket and the coxswains running down beach at Whitesands to scramble into their boats.

With no Rules whatsoever there was a Porthgain fishing boat that was deliberately causing rough water and wake near the Solva and Newport boats to slow them down. In the end, I think the Newport team did finish first, despite the unsporting behaviour of the Porthgain lobster men. It was no wonder Des Harries at Porthgain did not want an organising committee. The Porthgain boys had their own ideas of how to win the races even if it could not be done fairly. To be fair I only observed this in the very first Round Ramsey Race. I think the Porthgain rowers themselves may have told the offending skipper to not do it again. It was some years before the Longboat races became regulated in a manner that I had wanted at its concept. Despite minor setbacks this sea rowing sport in Wales has been the fastest growing sport, for each year, throughout its four decade history. I see in the last few years that Porthgain has acquired a clinker wooden built 6 oared gig . This means that these new class boats would be able to compete with the Isles of Scilly pilot gig regattas.

**Celtic Longboat, Mixed team from New Quay in 2012.**

The traditional rowing boats used at Newport were the three boats used for setting the seine nets for salmon in the bay. The Parrog boat was the No 1 boat called the "Seaweed Boat", as it was used to collect seaweed when not seine netting. Number 2 boat was called the "Woollen Boat" as the crew would consist of men working at the Wool Mill in the town. The Number 3 Boat was the "Heather Boat" as all the men came from the mountainside. These would be sturdy clinker built wooden row boats, but probably a lot larger than the four oared **Danny Boy.** Not particularly fast but comfortable to row and heavy. Once maximum speed obtained they would keep going forever. One boat **Danny Boy**, was still being used by the local boys in the Down River Race in 1975. It was reputed to be well over 100 years old then. Today it is still brought out to compete in the Dinas Head Challenge Race.

Reflecting on the name of this boat, does conjure up an affectionate Irish name. This is not surprising as it may have been built around 1850 when many of the coasting smacks built in Newport would regularly trade with Ireland. However it is not an Irish boat, its shape and construction, to me looks distinctly Newport made . Anyone knowing the shape of the Youghal rowing boat, with a beamier fore-quarter than aft, will understand what I am talking about.

From 1980's sea rowing with a one design boat then took off . The Griffiths brothers from Newport although in their late 30's were experienced and trained hard for the inaugural races of the " Cwch Hir". The Newport men's team was unbeatable for the next four years, they had, after all, had three generations of Griffiths brothers rowing in such races. Newport rowing team were one of the first teams to winter train properly for the summer rowing events. Norman Thomas, steward at the Boat Club, was instrumental in supporting the training, obtaining rowing machines and sending the Newport and Dinas boys to row race competitions in England. Because Newport boy's were rowing fit and familiar with competing in races of more than an hour, they did very well in all the long distance races they took part in.

With people trying to squeeze the Longboats into a lesser beam and starting to have moving seats, and outrigger the rowlock positions; it took the organisers about five years before they could appreciate Class Rules and the need for them. By commencing the whole sport unconventionally, without rules and without anyone knowing about sea rowing did help to get more people involved. I have to admit that my desire to have stringent regulations and standardisation from day one may have restricted its appeal in the early days and hindered, rather than aided the unbelievable growth in the sport.

When the Celtic Longboat Races started the only sea rowing Club in Wales was at Penarth. Some of the Sea Scouts competed against each other but there was very little rowing done around the coast. The Friday night rowing of traditional pilot gigs at St Mary's, Isles of Scilly was the only place in the British Isles where one could see traditional craft being raced. The St Mary's gigs were pilot gigs rowed by six oarsmen not four like the Longboat. The Porthgain Rowing Club now has a wooden six man gig, built in Cornwall, and have competed at the World Gig championships in the Isles of Scilly. The Porthgain, Solva and Newport lads were to change the sea rowing scene in Wales forever. Over the next 20 years, this revival of sea rowing and competition developed out of all proportion. Every port along the Welsh coast wanted at least one boat; one for the Men's team and one for the Ladies. Each coastal village started rowing training for Men's, Ladies, Mixed and Junior teams. A single specification boat was designed with a £100,000 Sportlot Grant in 1999, and the name Celtic Longboat given as the standard name. Dale Sailing Company produced a one design, GRP, fixed seat rowing boat based on the Pembrokeshire Longboat, which is now the standard for the sport. Since the Celtic one design started it is now estimated that there are 60 row boats competing each year around the entire Welsh coast.

A North Wales League commenced in 2003 and Celtic Longboats are now a feature down the entire West Coast of Wales. In North Wales, their most prestigious race is an annual event over a 14 mile course through the Menai Straits. In West Wales the premier event is the Dinas Head Challenge. A marathon 90 mile event with 12 rowers in each team, is crossing St George's Channel, Arklow to Aberystwyth. Named the Celtic Challenge, and competed for every two years. It started with n 1989 with Aberystwyth Lifeboat RNLI teams doing it to raise money for charity. Celtic, Pembrokeshire longboats and Irish gigs take part. Each boat is 24 feet (8m) long and has 4 fixed seats and one cox. Rowers can be changed and substituted at any stage of the race which usually lasts 17 to 24 hours. That is faster than most sailing boats can sail it. The Guinness Book of Records has recorded it as the longest competitive rowing race.

Today Celtic Long boats compete each year for the Dinas Head Challenge an 8 mile rowing race from Fishguard to Newport. The winning boats complete the course in less than an hour, meaning they row at a speed of over 9 mph (8 knots) . 32 boats competed in 2014. It is probably one of the most popular sea rowing events in the Welsh calendar. With the Dinas Head Challenge; it could be said that Newport has maintained it rowing race tradition for nearly 200 years.

While I was studying Newport losses I happened to come across other Cardigan registered vessels that were lost. Here are some of them which will aid those researching the Cardigan ships. Some of them may have had Newport shareholders.

In November 1801, the 32 ton Newport owned **Peggy** stranded (and may have been wrecked) on the north side of Cardigan Bar. She was on a journey with salt from Liverpool to Bristol but had gone into the shelter of her home port due to bad weather. Grounding on the way out her valuable cargo attracted great attention, including the interest of the Custom's men. The Captain had to appear before the Sessions to testify that the loss of the cargo which was subject to considerable salt duty, had been lost due to the elements.

"The smack **Brothers**, of Cardigan, bound from Portmadoc to Cardiff, with a cargo of slates, stranded on the north side of Skomer Island at 6 a.m. on Tuesday morning during a very heavy gale. The vessel is a total wreck. At low water she can be reached, therefore her cargo will be saved. No lives were lost" *South Wales Daily News 12th March 1891 p.6* Glen Johnson records a **Brothers** Smack of 46 tons. Built 1848 Cardigan. 1892 Wrecked. Probably same vessel.

FISHERMAN LOST IN CARDIGAN BAY On Friday morning last about 5 o'clock a retired seaman named David Jones, residing at the village of Moelgrove, went in a sailing boat to the bay, with the intention of fishing. He never returned, and though the coast from St. David's Head to New Quay has been searched no trace of the boat or occupant has...(*South Wales Daily News 7th July 1899 News p.6)*

CARDIGAN. THE LATE GALE.-During the gale that occurred on Sunday night a vessel is supposed to have been wrecked in the bay. On Monday morning a boat named the Phryne was washed on shore, as well as many splinters, spars, (be. of a ship. The smack **Mary**, laden with culm, was stranded at Cybwr, a headland at the mouth of the Tivy. The **Ellen Owen** and the] **Commerce** were both stranded at Fishguard....(*The Pembrokeshire Herald and General Advertiser 15th November 1872.)*

SUPPOSED LOSS OF A VESSEL IN CARDIGAN BAY. On Saturday, a large vessel, flying a flag of distress, was observed by the coast-guard lookout at Penrhyn Castle, about a mile and a half outside the limits of Cardigan Bay. A rocket was fired to call together the lifeboat crew, who responded without delay. Before the boat, however, was launched, the vessel had disappeared in a heavy squall. It is supposed the crew were all lost, as even if they had taken to their boats it is not probable that they could have lived in such a sea as was running at the time. ( Seen in *South Wales Daily News 18th October 1886* ).

"The Great Western Railway Company's mail steamer Great Western (Captain Guy), whilst on her passage to Waterford, on Tuesday morning, ran down the sloop, **Penryn Castle** of Cardigan. The accident occurred off St. Ann's Head, about a quarter to four o'clock. Captain Guy" …*South Wales Daily News 4th October 1873*. **Penryn Castle.** 44 ton built 1839 Lawrenny. 1840, Captain William Lewis.

SHIPPING DISASTERS. A CARDIGAN VESSEL WRECKED. A Holyhead telegram reports that during a terrible gale yesterday morning the **Elizabeth Davies,** which sailed from Cardigan on Thursday, was wrecked at Cymmerau, a dangerous spot on the Anglesey coast. A man named Richard Harris was drowned, but Stephen James, the captain, succeeded in swimming ashore. ( *South Wales Echo 24th December 1898.*)

WRECKED AT NEWPORT PEMBROKESHIRE
The 23 ton Sloop **Jenny** built at New Quay in 1792 was lost off Newport with her cargo valued £150. Her ship's papers were also lost so we can assume she foundered on her voyage from Milford to Cardigan. The date was 22nd October 1840.
*(Via Donald Davies of Cardigan, County Echo)*

SHIPPING CASUALTIES. During the gales of the past week several ships belonging to this district have been lost or damaged. The **Maria Anna.**, Mr Thomas Daniel, Sea View-place, master and owner, sunk in two fathoms water off Cronane Point, Killorglin, but the crew were .saved. The **Mary Eliza**, schooner, of Cardigan, John Evans, Borth, master, from Aberdovey to Londonderry with slates, has been driven ashore near Pontlogan, Wigtonshire, Scotland. The master and boy were saved by jumping upon the rocks, but the mate and an able seaman, supposed to belong to Aberdovey were drowned. The vessel is expected to become a total loss. The **Ellen Anne,** schooner, Mr Jones, New Quay, master, from Trefort for Western Point with boulders, has been greatly damaged by having been in collision with the tug **United Kingdom** of Liverpool. She became unmanageable and had to be towed into port. The schooner **John James,** Richard Clayton, Aberystwth, master, from Porthdinorwic to Macduff with slates, has put into Belfast Lough having lost bulwarks, boat and sustained other damage. (*The Cambrian News and Merionethshire Standard 27th February 1885 News p.5 )*

…Smack in Distress. CARDIGAN LIFEBOAT TO THE RESCUE The vessel in distress in Cardigan Bay on Sunday morning proved to be the smack **Ann,** of Beaumaris, owned by Mr. David Luke, of Newport, Pem. She had a cargo of culm from Milford to Newport, and was,* blown out of her course by the wind, with the loss of all her sails. The weather was thick with rain squalls. She was first seen at 1.45 a.m…(*Evening Express, Special Edition 22nd October 1906)*

SHIPPING AND MAIL NEWS. The **Ruth,** schooner, of Cardigan, from Fishguard Roads for Swansea, with culm, stranded on Cardigan bar on the 18th inst. ( *South Wales Daily News 26th March 1872)*

**Mary Eliza,** schooner, of Cardigan, has been assisted into Ramsgate by boatmen, with loss of anchor and 80 fathoms of Chain. (*Aberystwith Observer . 6th November 1880)*

CASUALTIES. having been in collision. **Rachel**, sloop, of Cardigan, Jenkins, from Llangranog for Milford, in ballast, foundered off Cardigan Harbour on the 6th inst. crew saved. *(South Wales Daily News 11th October 1873 News p.4)*

CARDIGAN VESSEL LOST. ALL HANDS GONE. A Dover correspondent telegraphing on Saturday says :-There appears to be little doubt that the small Welsh schooner **Leander** has been lost in the Channel with all hands, a lifeboat having been picked up by a Dover tug with one oar floating near bearing the name **Leander,** Cardigan, The vessel is registered at Lloyds as 72 tons, and owned by J. Jones, of Cardigan. *( The Cambrian)*

SHIPPING DISASTERS. CARDIGAN VESSEL WRECKED. A SEAMAN DROWNED. A Holyhead telegram reports that during a terrible gale yesterday morning the **Elizabeth Davies,** which sailed from Cardigan on Thursday, was wrecked at Cymmerau, a dangerous spot on the Anglesey coast. A man named Richard Harris was drowned, but Stephen James, the captain, succeeded in swimming ashore. *(South Wales Daily News (Third Edition) 24th December 1898)* .She was a 28 ton Smack built in Cardigan in 1868.

LOSS OF A CARDIGAN VESSEL AND CREW. There is now no doubt, it is said, that the crew of the vessel **Princess Royal,** which went ashore near Camden Fort, at the entrance to Cork harbour, on Christmas Eve, were drowned. The vessel herself became a total wreck. She was believed to belong to Cardigan, and was laden with cement from Crosshaven. (*The Cambrian News and Merionethshire Standard 3 January 1879).*

LOSS OF A CARDIGAN VESSEL. THE CAPTAIN MAD. - The schooner **Juliana,** bound from Fecamp to London in ballast, was run ashore at Hastings about midnight on Monday, by the crew, who state that shortly after leaving port the captain and owner, Mr. John Davies, of St. Dogmells, showed signs of insanity, and, when off Hastings, attempted to jump overboard. He was brought ashore and charged with being a wandering lunatic, and with attempting suicide. He was sent to an asylum. A Lloyd's telegram says that the vessel will become a total wreck. It will be remembered that the **Juliana.** was laying at the quay for some time last summer. *(The Cardigan Observer and General Advertiser for the Counties of Cardigan Carmarthen and Pembroke. 17th December 1887.)*

FISHGUARD SMACK SUNK. CREW SAVED. A telegram has just arrived at Fishguard stating that the smack **Lord Exmouth** sank on Saturday afternoon in Ramsey Sound. The crew consisted of two men, who were both saved. Their names are Captain David James, of Wallis Street, Fishguard, who was. also the owner of the vessel, and the mate, William Edwards, of Dinas Cross, Pembrokeshire. The vessel, which was insured, was of 35 tons register, and at the time of the disaster was bound from Hook to Fishguard with a cargo of culm. *(Seen South Wales Daily News 17th October 1898)*

FRENCH KETCH WRECKED "The French ketch **Adolphe,** with a cargo of onions from Roscoff for Cardigan, went ashore at St. Dogmaels during Thursday night, and is a total wreck. The crew and passengers are safe. I VESSEL OVERDUE. The ketch **Margaret and Anne,** of Fishguard, is much overdue, and fears are entertained for her safety. The owners are making inquiries around the Welsh coast." *Seen Evening Express 21*[st] *August 1909. Page 2.*

BEARHAVEN, Feb 12.1852 The **Eliza**, Larod, of Milford, hence for Limerick, with coal, was totally wrecked, last evening, on the Carrigavaddra Rock crew saved. Owned by Thomas Searne of Fishguard. (*Liverpool Mercury, Tuesday, February 17, 1852)*

The **Harmony,** Schooner from the Shannon to Gloucester was struck by a heavy sea during a gale on the 17th of March 1867 which carried away her boats, &c. After this the sea made clean breaches over her. On the 19th the **S.S.Darien** bore up and took the crew off, the **Harmony** then being in a sinking state. The first boat the Darien sent out was accidentally capsized, and three men were drowned the second boat succeeded in saving the whole of the crew five. *Board Of Trade Wreck Reports 1867* The steamer **Darien,** Captain E. S. Haram, belonging to the West India and Pacific Steam Ship Company, from Port-au- Prince for Liverpool with a general cargo put into Valentia harbour on Wednesday short of coals. She had lost two officers and one man whilst rescuing the screw of the schooner **Harmony of Cardigan** which had been abandoned 60 miles S.W. of Dursies. (*Liverpool Mercury etc Friday, March 22,1867)*

**Rescue by Newport Lifeboat 1889.**

The South Wales Daily News on 9th October 1889 describes what happened. It was one of the few rescues performed by the Newport Lifeboat.

The schooner **Reliance** (built 1865 of 77 tons) left Wexford her home port on a Sunday morning in ballast, bound for Newport Monmouthshire. When in St George's Channel she was overtaken by a storm. She was dismasted and a huge sea carried away her jib boom. This meant that she could not sail properly and required attention. Another vessel saw her plight and came over to help. They thought the crew wanted to abandon so came as near as they could and threw a life buoy and line across. One of the crew who endeavoured to take advantage of it, failed to catch it and was drowned. The others declined the proffered service and remained on their vessel. About 9.30 pm on Monday night the vessel driven helplessly before the storm, arrived some two and a half miles outside Newport, Pembrokeshire and anchored there. Responding to signals of distress the Newport Lifeboat crew were mustered. As many of the proper crew that could be mustered arrived as well as keen volunteers. Amongst those that manned the lifeboat were eight volunteers described mostly as landsmen. They rowed with great difficulty in the dark through the heavy ground sea and reached the stricken schooner at about 3.00 am. They rescued the master, the mate and an ordinary seaman. On account of the fierceness of the weather the Life Boat had to put a sail up and run for Cardigan. "Great praise is due to Captain D.Evans, Captain Llewelyn Davies and a number of young men (18 to 20 years old) who volunteered their Services." The schooner did not sink and was recovered. In fact with the same Captain T. Hutchinson and 4 crew the **Reliance** was lost in a collision in Chapel Bay, Milford Haven, some two and a half year later.

**INDEX (Alphabetical) of Newport (Pembrokeshire) ships.**

**This is a list of Newport Pembrokeshire vessels mainly from 1760 to 1860. Most are built in Newport, but those built elsewhere are included as they had Newport share holders or captains.**

Adroit built Newport 1842 Schooner 72 ton.
Agenoria built Newport 1834 Schooner 117 ton lost 1879
Aid built Cardigan 1829 Smack 25 ton lost 1869.
Agnes of Portsmouth built Newport 1832 Schooner 89 tons
Alert built Newport 1835 Sloop 33 ton lost 1881
Anne built Newport 1842 Brig 161 ton lost 1874.
Ann built elsewhere 1841 Smack 27 ton
Ann and Betsey built Newport (Mon?) 1833 Smack 22 ton
Ann and Betsey built Newport 1837 Smack 27 ton scrapped 1920.
Ann and Mary built Newport 1762 Smack 17 ton lost 1873
Anna Maria built Aberdovey 1784 Schooner 47 ton lost 1795
Ant built Newport 1816 Brig/Snow 122 ton lost 1821
Ardent built Newport 1817 Schooner 125 ton
Ardent built Newport 1800 Snow 120 ton lost 1833.
Artuose built Newport 1814 Brig 157 ton lost 1876
Bee built Cardigan or Newport 1784 Sloop 66 ton
Bee built at Newport 1785 Sloop 70 ton lost 1821
Benjamin of Milford built Newport 1785 Sloop 64 ton
Betsey built Newport 1827 Sloop 24 ton
Betsey of Bristol built Newport 1784 Brig 150 ton lost 1819.
Betsey of Milford built Newport 1787 Sloop 54 ton lost 1820
Betty built Newport 1777 Sloop 24 ton lost 1829
Britannia built Cei Bach 1776 Sloop 19 ton
Britannia built Barmouth 1779 Sloop 35 ton lost 1822 (?)
Brothers built Newport 1826 Schooner 99 ton lost c. 1865
Cambria built Abercastle 1793 Sloop 25 ton.

**Newport Vessels,** Built or Owned. (continued)

Castle Malgwyn built Cardigan Brig 100 ton lost 1833
Catherine built Newport 1797 23 ton lost 1896
Catherine built 1784 Sloop 21 ton lost 1793
Charlotte built Newport 1798 Sloop 36 ton lost 1835.
Charlotte built Newport 1804 Schooner 86 ton Charlotte built Newport 1824 Schooner 81 ton
Claudia built Newport 1835 Schooner 135 ton lost 1871
Commerce built Carmarthen 1800 Sloop 35 ton lost 1873
Connium built elsewhere 1840 Sloop 23 ton lost 1872
Culloden built Newport 1804 Schooner 83 ton lost 1825
Darling not sure where built but Sloop sank in 1821
David built Newport 1813 Sloop 35 ton .
David built Newport 1830 Smack 26 ton lost 1882
Diligence built Newport 1814 Brig 100 ton lost 1840
Dinas built Abercastle 1820 Sloop 38 ton
Dolphin built in Newport 1787 Sloop 59 ton lost 1803
Dove built Aberystwyth 1783 Smack 36 ton lost 1817
Eleanor built Newport 1795 Sloop 51 ton lost 1823.
Eliza built Wales 1800 Brig 147 ton lost 1856
Eliza built Foreign Brig 135 ton Dinas owned
Eliza built Newport 1847 Brig 197 ton Regis Aberystwyth .
Eliza built Gloucester 1822 Smack 16 ton lost 1863.
Eliza built Milford 1827 Brigantine 97 tons. Lost 1863
Eliza built 1827 not Newport, Schooner, 160 ton Lost 1833 Eliza Edwards built Newport (Gwent?) 1839 Schooner 147 tons
Elizabeth built Newport 1793 Sloop 54 tons
Elizabeth built Newport 1826 Brigantine 108 /97 tons
Elizabeth built Newport 1826 Schooner 85 ton
Elizabeth built 1839 Sloop 27 ton lost 1874
Elizabeth Anne built Newport 1835 Schooner 126 ton lost 1871
Elizabeth and Mary built Newport 1792 Sloop 60 ton lost 1828

## Newport Vessels (continued)

Excel   built 1854 but not at Newport   Brig  213 ton
Excel   built 1853 but not at Newport   Brig   221 ton
Exley built Hull 1840 Sloop 29 ton  lost 1871.
Expedition built Kidwelly 1809 Sloop 35 ton lost 1837 or 1822
Fair Briton built Newport   1785  Sloop 45 ton
Fanny built Newport 1786 Sloop 33 ton
Fanny Anne built Newport 1801 Sloop  22 ton lost 1841.
Fanny and Mary built Newport 1787 Sloop
Fanny and Mary  built Newport 1807 Sloop.
Felicity   built elsewhere  Brig of Milford
Flora built Newport 1795 Sloop 27 ton lost 1829
Fly built elsewhere pre 1810 Smack 23 ton  lost 1839
Frances built Newport 1830 Schooner 71 ton
Frances built Aberporth 1808 Sloop 33 ton
Friendship built Newport 1817 Brig /Snow 83 ton lost 1819
Gleaner  ( ?)   Schooner or Brig  88 ton
Grace  built Newport 1828   Schooner 103 ton lost c. 1870
Harmony built Newport 1829 Schooner 95 ton lost c. 1882
Hope built elsewhere in 1802 Schooner 85 ton
Hope built Newport 1805 Sloop 21 ton
Hope of Fishguard built Newport 1812 Sloop 29 ton
Hope built Newport 1826   Snow  112 ton
Hope  built Cardigan or Newport 1825 Brig  129 tons
Hope not built at Newport 1813 Brig 155 ton
Hope   built Newport 1827 Snow/ Brig 182 ton
Hopewell built New Quay 1810  Sloop 18 ton lost 1852
Hopewell built Cardigan 1826 Sloop 71 ton lost 1833
Jane of Goodwick built Newport 1790 Sloop 70 ton lost 1833.
Jane built Fishguard 1832  Sloop  32 ton
Jane built Newport 1837 Schooner 78 ton lost 1879
Jane and Catherine, built 1837 not Newport, 1837 Sloop 29 ton

## Newport Vessels  (continued)

Jane and Margaret built Llansanffraid  Sloop  29 ton lost 1859
John built Bridgwater 1770 Schooner 70 ton lost 1805
John built Milford or Dinas 1828 Sloop 28 ton lost 1867
John built Newport 1789 Sloop 35 ton lost 1831
Jolly built at Newport 1786 Sloop 24 ton
Jupiter built Newport 1802 Sloop 64 ton lost 1843
Keturah built Newport 1787 Brigantine 113 ton lost after 1805
Lord Nelson built Newport 1782 Snow 107 ton lost 1835
Lord Nelson built Newport 1802 Snow  109 ton lost 1840.
Lady Day  built Newport  1825  Schooner  128 ton lost 1837
Little Speedwell built Newport 1776 Smack 18 ton
Lovely Peggy built Newport 1787 Sloop  29 ton lost 1819
Margaret built Milford 1830 Schooner or Snow 128 ton lost 1836
Maria built New Quay 1849 Schooner 64 ton
Maria Eliza  1822  Brig 87 ton ? Newport. Mon?
Maria and Anne built Newport  1830   Sloop 65 ton
Maria and Martha built Fishguard 1808 Sloop  69 ton
Martha built Appledore Devon 1819 Brig 123 ton Martha built Newport 1786 Sloop 29 ton
Mary  rebuilt Newport 1773 Sloop 24 ton
Mary built Newport 1785  Sloop 48 tons
Mary built Newport 1819 Sloop 53 ton lost 1853
Mary built Newport 1781 Sloop 21 ton
Mary built Newport 1783 Brigantine 53 ton
Mary built Aberayron 1778 Sloop  26 ton
Mary and Eleanor  1818  Schooner 122 ton.
Mary and Eliza built Carmarthen 1824 Sloop 129 ton
Mary Anne built Newport 1810  Sloop 28 ton lost 1859
Mary Ann built Newport 1816  Sloop 23 ton lost 1906
Mary and Margaret  built Kincardine 1807 Brig 131 ton lost 1847
Mathildis  built New Quay 1842 Brig   133 ton lost 1859
Menai  built Newport 1792 Sloop 70 ton lost 1825

## Newport Vessels (continued)

Mermaid prize in 1777 Sloop  28 ton & 21 ton
Milford built St Dogmaels 1788 Sloop 40 ton lost 1801.
Minerva built |Newport 1811 Brigantine  102 ton.
Minerva built Newport 1821 Brig 102 ton
Nancy built Newport 1798 Sloop 64 ton
Nancy 1785 Sloop 19 ton
Nancy built Newport 1786 Sloop 29 ton lost 1825.
Neptune of Milford built Newport 1797 Brigantine 60 ton.
Nightingale  built Newport 1778   Sloop 40 ton lost 1811 Oak built 1840 but not in Newport , Flat  33 ton 1840
Ocean of Llanelly built Newport 1832 Brig 121 ton lost 1861
Ocean  Not sure where built . Brig  106 ton
Perfect of Youghal built Newport 1836 Schooner 124 tons.
Peggy  built Newport 1787   Sloop 21 ton
Peggy  built 1790 Wales 32 tons lost 1801
Pheasant    built New Quay 1829  Sloop  30 ton
Pheasant    built elsewhere in 1837 Sloop 25 ton
Phoebe (Phebe) built Newport 1839  Brig 123 ton lost 1843.
Phoenix  built Newport 1785 Sloop 24 ton
Prince of Wales  1786 Sloop  49 ton

Princess Royal built Newport 1803 Brigantine 95 ton.

Providence built Newport 1777 Sloop 28 ton lost 1807
Providence built Newport 1783 Sloop 24 ton lost 1814
Providence built Newport 1787 Sloop 25 ton lost 1819.
Providence built Newport 1826 Sloop 28 ton
Providence  built Newport  1841   Schooner 70 ton
Reform   built Newport 1831 Sloop 14 ton.
Richard & Mary built Pembroke Dock 1848 Smack 18 ton.
Rowlands of Newport Mon. Brig 102 ton  1811.
Rose built Newport 1773 Sloop 22 ton
Royal Recovery built Leith 1789 Brig 82 ton lost 1832.
Samson  Brig of Newport  built before 1826.
Sarah built Cardigan 1842 Schooner 124 ton lost 1865.

## Newport Vessels (continued)

Shannon Packet built Low Island, Ireland Sloop 37 ton
Samson built Newport 1800 Brigantine 121 ton lost after 1839
Speculator built Aberystwyth 1804 Sloop 76/72 ton
Speedwell built Newport 1782 Sloop 24 ton lost 1810
Speedwell of Llanelly built Newport 1765 lost after 1788
Speedwell built Newport 1788 Sloop 13 ton
Speedwell built Merionethshire 1780 Sloop 42 ton lost 1840
Susannah built Carmarthen 1782 Sloop 29 ton lost 1812.
Swallow built Barmouth 1783 Sloop 30 ton lost 1809
Swift built Newport 1825 Sloop 39 ton maybe lost 1841
Taff of Twenty Two built Cardiff 1822 Sloop 26 ton lost 1851.
Teifi Lass built Cardigan 1840 Sloop 33 ton lost 1856
True Briton built Aberporth 1793 Sloop 15 ton lost 1856
Two Brothers built Newport prior 1787 Sloop 47 ton lost 1867
Twins built Newport 1790 Sloop 22 ton.
Valiant built Newport 1812 Brig 144 ton.
Venerable built Newport 1815 Brig 130 ton lost circa 1829
Venus of Cardigan built at Newport 1794 Sloop 35 ton
Victoria Brig 458 ton
Victory built Newport 1812 Brigantine 118 ton lost 1819.
William and Ann built Newport 1790 Sloop 88 ton lost 1833.

In 1839 **Eliza Edwards** a schooner 147 tons was built at Newport but went into the Youghal Register in Ireland. I have not yet determined if this schooner was built in Newport, Gwent (Monmouthshire) or Newport Pembrokeshire.

From the list above we can see that at least 84 vessels were built at Newport in the years 1760 to 1860. Although Lloyds Register of shipping does not distinguish which Newport some ships were built the majority built before 1825 were at Pembrokeshire. The above list has been compiled from the Cardigan Registers where 95% of the vessels built at Newport Pembrokeshire were first registered.

This is the Amlwch schooner **Desdemona** managed by Cricieth owners. Losing her jib and foresails in a storm she became unmanageable forcing her captain, H.Williams, to run her ashore onto Newport beach, a place he knew well. Her five crew were saved by rocket apparatus. The effects of a two day storm were battering the beach and the vessel pounded heavily opening up her bottom planks. The **Desdemona**, 79 feet long, was built at Aberystwyth in 1874 and wrecked on Newport Beach on 11th February 1906. With a cargo of clay she was on her way from Poole to Liverpool. After the crew had been rescued the cargo was discharged. As far as I can ascertain she was dismantled on the beach. The firebricks to be seen on the sand bar at very low water at the other end of the beach may be something to do with a cargo from this schooner.

# References

E. A. Lewis, Welsh Port Books, 1550- 1603.
Transactions of the Honourable Society of Cymmrodorion, 1926.
Nooks and Corners of Pembrokeshire 1895 Timmins
Deadly Perils, Peter B S Davies 1992.
NLW, Llwyngwair mss 15274, 15324, 15333; NLW, Lucas mss 99, 414-18, 3086, 3087.
Shipwrecks Around Wales, Vol One 1987. Tom Bennett
www.rhiw.com/y_mor/adeiladu_llongau/pwllheli.htm
http://www.nationalhistoricships.org.uk/register/136/garlandstone
www.dyfedarchaeology.org.uk/HLC/newportandcarningli/newport.htm
www.glen-johnson.co.uk/cardigan-st-dogmaels-ships-and-captains/
www.newport-pembs.co.uk/index.php/prehistory-of-newport-and-nevern
Archifdy Ceredigion Archives. Ref: ADX/1191. Reference: [GB 0212] ADX/1191 Title: Cardigan Shipping Register Date(s): [original 1786-1813] Scope and Content: Transcript of the Statutory register of Shipping, Cardigan 1786-1813. Original is in Pembrokeshire Archives, Haverfordwest.
ceredigion.gov.uk/utilities/action/act_download.cfm?mediaid=19166 &langtoken=eng)
http://newspapers.library.wales/
Tovey, Ron. "A Chronology of Bristol Channel Shipwrecks" (PDF).
www.maritimearchives.co.uk/lloyds-register.html
Cemais, Dillwyn Miles, Haverfordwest, 1998.
Echoes and Shadows: tales and traditions of Newport and Nevern, Brian John, Newport, 2008.
Carningli: land and people, Brian John, Newport, 2008.
Cylchgrawn Hanes Cymru, Volume 19, Issues 3-4
http://daibach-welldigger.blogspot.co.uk/2012/07/saint-brynach-and-mountain-of-angels.html

*www.irishwrecksonline.net/Lists/CorkListG.htm*

**Methodology of information collection used in this book.**
Pre 1990 I made a database of all vessels that were built at Newport using material collected by Robin Craig and my own research from the Cardigan Customs Registers. The Milford Registers, where some of the later Newport built vessels were documented were not systematically looked through as they were not available in Pembrokeshire at that time. The prime original notes were digitally indexed on my computer using an early version of Dbase 3. Fortunately I printed the lists alphabetically and in date order of all the Newport vessels that I had at that time, before making new databases when Windows software started. Using these indexes I have added information from my own extensive card indexes on Welsh wrecks. Other information has been added from the Welsh Newspapers online and from Larn and Larn Welsh Index Volume 5. Cross- checking dates of loss was done using the wreck list of at the back of a book ***Dive Pembrokeshire Shipwrecks*** by Greg Evans ISBN 0951211498, 9780951211496

**About the Author:** Tom Bennett (1947- ) has written a variety of books about Welsh maritime matters. He is best known for his "Sea Guide to Pembrokeshire", a pilot book about the coastline that he has spent a lifetime exploring. Two recent titles "The Silver Dollars of Rhossili" solves the Gower mystery of how treasure found its way on to the sands of Llangennith Beach. The other "Ty Gwyn and the Bronze Bell Wreck" investigates the historic shipwreck discovered near Barmouth and why the ship lost had no name. Tom is now a landlubber researching the Neolithic in Pembrokeshire. He has discovered evidence of not only where Bluestones were quarried but which North Pembrokeshire beach they set sail (or rather rowed out) from.

Look out for his latest books on his website
**Shipwrecksforwalkers.co.uk.**

This book was compiled, written and typed by Tom Bennett. Although ©
Tom Bennett 2018 you are welcome to use parts of the content, provided appropriate wording such as extract from " **Maritime History of Newport, Pembrokeshire" by Tom Bennett,** is included as an acknowledgement.
If you would like to make any comments, additions or corrections please get in touch. My email is Happyfish42@hotmail.com.

Diver Greg Evans recovering a water jug from the wreck of the *David* in Ramsey Sound.
The *David* was one of the sloops built for coastal work by the Havard shipbuiders of Newport, described in this book.